CREATED
FOR
SUCCESSFUL
LIVING

Wee

Phil 2:13

CREATED
FOR
SUCCESSFUL
LIVING

BY

WILFRED KENT

TODAY'S WORLD MINISTRIES
INTERNATIONAL PUBLISHERS

Unless otherwise indicated, all scripture quotations are taken from the King James Version of the Bible.

Second Edition, First Impression, 1994

Created For Successful Living
ISBN 0-620-17351-3
Copyright © 1994 TWM International Publishers

TWM International Publishers   Tel: 303/220-9266
P O Box 1000   Fax: 303/220-8246
Parker, Colorado, 80134, USA

P O Box 1300   Tel: 204/326-3477
Steinbach, Manitoba, R0A.2A0, Canada

P O Box 59, Alberton, 1450   Tel: 011/907-9397
Republic of South Africa   Fax: 011/907-9273

Printed and bound by Sigma Press (Pty) Ltd, Pretoria

Dedication

I dedicate this book to my parents, Mike and Hazel, who "loaned" their only son to the Lord at birth, and made every effort to ensure his calling.

Thank you Mom and Dad.

Acknowledgement

Special recognition is given to those who so tirelessly dedicated their talents in making this publication possible. This includes:

Ronell Swartz   -   Proof-reading and Editing
Greg Riddle   -   Cover design
Janelle Michie   -   Type-setting

and the many people whose life experiences have served as notable examples and illustrations.

Table of Keys

Key		Page
1	Created with purpose	1
2	Thinking controls being	7
3	The end result	12
4	Seven diseases of the soul	16
5	How to stay well and be happy	23
6	Lucky or jinxed?	29
7	Trouble can be a friend	36
8	Surgery of the soul	43
9	Poison for the mind	47
10	A happy spirit is like medicine	52
11	Potential wrapped in human skin	56
12	Hypnotic powers which bind	60
13	What happened to sound thinking?	65
14	Slave to the ordinary	69
15	An antidote for illness	73
16	Imagination: a creative force	78
17	Physician, heal thyself	85
18	Skeletons in your closet	90
19	Exposure to a sick society	97
20	Not cure but deliverance	102
21	Who in the world am I?	107
22	How to conquer depression	117
23	Thy speech betrays thee	123
24	Thinking can be a waste	129

Table of Keys

Key   **Page**

25   Causes for a negative attitude 133
26   Smile and kwityerbelyakin! 138
27   How to achieve mediocrity 141
28   The quagmire of public opinion 145
29   How to develop character 151
30   Simple formulas for success 156
31   Sick standards for self-image 161
32   A butterfly or a worm? 165
33   Pride is too expensive 169
34   What you eat is what you get 173
35   Poor Charlie! 179
36   Verbal jousting 183
37   Incompatibility or inflexibility 188
38   Marriage can be a pain 193
39   Love is a decision 197
40   Reversals can be beneficial 201
41   Project "new start!" 205

KEY 1   CREATED WITH PURPOSE

Do you realize that you are not here at this juncture of time and space by accident? You are a distinctive object of God's handiwork. You are His unique workmanship and here by divine appointment. We live in a universe which is sustained by law and order, and governed by cause and effect relationships to its finest detail. It is inconceivable to think that mankind, who is the highest form of intelligent life, is but a product of chance. It is unthinkable to suggest that man is but the evolutionary development of primeval slime. Such assumption requires the blind fanaticism of a religious zealot. It is impossible to suppose that man's purpose for being cannot be known, and that the events of every day are but consequences of random happenings. Those who teach this philosophy see life as an impossible enigma, and to them existence itself is an incomprehensible riddle. They see life as an impenetrable mystery. Andre Maurois, the noted French biographer and author, summarized this well when he wrote:

"The universe is indifferent. Who created it? Why are we here on this puny mud heap spinning in infinite space? I have not the slightest idea and I am quite convinced that no one has..."

King David had a much better understanding of life. He described life in terms of purpose and grand design. Make a study of his explanation in Psalm 8:3-6. It is a source of encouragement to all who read it.

"When I consider the heavens, the works of thy fingers, the moon and the stars, which thou hast ordained; What is man that thou art mindful of him? and the son of man, that thou visitest him? For thou hast made him a little lower than the angels (Elohim, meaning God) and hast crowned him with glory and honour. Thou madest him to have dominion over the works of thy hands; thou hast put all things under his feet."

How would you answer the following thought-provoking questions: "What is your purpose for being? Why are you here? Is your life worth it all? What eternal purpose do you fulfil? Is there any reason for your existence? Is the world any better because of your presence? What purpose and meaning does your life offer? Is there more to life than making it through to Friday?" Your answers could be life-changing. We all need to remember the Psalmist's declarations in the above passage.

1. WHAT IS MAN THAT YOU ARE MINDFUL OF HIM?

God is mindful of us. In other words, His mind is full of us. Can you comprehend the grand implications? He who created the universe, designed each planet and placed it in its designated orbit, is preoccupied with you and your well-being! Rather than being a product of chance, you are His distinctive workmanship, designed and programmed for *"good works"* and monitored by His mindful concern. This is clearly the import of Ephesians 2:10:

"For we are His workmanship, created in Christ Jesus unto good works, which God hath before ordained that we should walk in them."

Can you imagine God creating anything substandard? His workmanship is never slipshod! God does not operate a "Factory Warehouse Outlet" where he offers rejects at basement bargain prices. His quality control standards are high, and He always meets them!

2. WHO IS THE SON OF MAN THAT YOU VISITED HIM?

Do you remember a time when God actually visited man? He lived among us, visited our homes, ate our food and slept in our beds. Mary and Joseph knew him. The disciples knew him well. Mary called him Jesus, the disciples called Him Lord, and Peter declared: *"Thou art the Christ, the Son of the living God."* He is God come in human flesh!

"Behold, a virgin shall be with child, and shall bring forth a son, and they shall call his name Emmanuel, which being interpreted is, God with us." - Matthew 1:23

The Hebrew meaning of His name, Emmanuel, is revealing! *Immanu* means "among us". *El* is the abbreviation for Elohim, the word which means "God". (Isaiah 7:14; Matthew 1:21-23; John 1:1+13, 14-18; Revelation 3:14) All the Elohistic names of God are consummate in this name, Emmanuel. Jesus Christ is God incarnate, "God with us!" Isaiah foresaw this when he declared:

"For unto us a child is born (the body of Jesus was born of a woman), unto us a Son is given (Jesus, the Son of God, was given of the Father): and the government shall be upon his shoulder: and his name shall be called Wonderful, Counsellor, The mighty God, The everlasting Father, The Prince of Peace." - Isaiah 9:6

He visits us in the same manner today. If you stop long enough to look for him, you will find him. If you quieten yourself, you will hear his voice. In bodily form, He is Jesus Christ. In Spirit form He dwells in His temple made without hands, namely the body of every child of God! You will see Him reflected in the faces of those who love Him.

3. YOU MADE HIM A LITTLE LOWER THAN ANGELS

The word which is translated here as "angels" is "Elohim" in the original. It is used in Genesis 1:1-2 for the first time. It means GOD! *"In the beginning God (Elohim) created heaven and earth."* This is a direct reference to Jesus, but it is also true of us. As people in human flesh, neither you nor I were created in substandard form. We were created "...a little lower than God." Most of us have organized an erroneous hierarchy for life. It looks something like this:

God the Father
God the Son, Jesus Christ
God the Holy Spirit
The Angelic Host
Fallen Principalities and Powers
Man
Woman
Children
Conscious Life
Unconscious Existence

At the top of the pyramid is the Triune Godhead, followed by the angels, then the fallen angelic host which consists of principalities, powers and the demonic ranks. This in turn is directly followed by mankind: man, woman then child. Then comes the conscious life: beasts, birds, fish and creeping things, followed by the unconscious life which is the kingdom of all vegetation. At the bottom of this pyramid is the material world of rocks, metals and minerals.

This notion places mankind one brief step above a turkey and two short steps above a carrot. The following model is more accurate: firstly we have the Triune Godhead: Father, Son and Holy Ghost, the Three in One. This is followed by **mankind** ! We must once again underscore that we were created in His image, "a little lower than God." I don't know what this does for you, but I get excited. Angels, according to Hebrews 1:13-14, have been created and commissioned by God to minister unto us:

"... angels ... Are they not all ministering spirits, sent forth to minister for them who shall be heirs of salvation?"

And what about the angelic host who rebelled, left their first estate and became demons, principalities and powers of wickedness in high places? No one could answer this more clearly than God Himself, our Lord Jesus Christ:

"And he said unto them, I beheld Satan as lightening fall from heaven. Behold, I give you power to tread on (these) serpents and scorpions, and over all the power of the enemy: and nothing shall by any means hurt you." - Luke 10:18-19

This ranking has vast implications! One thing is certain, however, your life is not without purpose and meaning. The following hierarchy is more accurate:

The Godhead
Mankind - You!
Angelic Host
All Conscious Life
The Material Kingdom
All Fallen Creatures

4. YOU MADE HIM TO HAVE DOMINION

Don't ever succumb to the concept that you are a victim of circumstance! You are not a product of random happenings; just some inconsequential bark, drifting aimlessly and helplessly on a tide of fate. You have been given **dominion** over your lot in life. Do not be seduced by circumstances into abdicating your rights! You are not an emotional puppet which dances to the tugging of casual occurrence. Take charge of your life.

G N Clark, in his inaugural address at Cambridge, said, "There is no secret and no plan in history to be acknowledged..." I am sorry, Dr Clark, but I respectfully differ! History is full of meaning and the future is full of potential. Each day scintillates with expectancy. Furthermore, I am sitting on the cutting edge of all that is happening! What an enviable state.

"Before I formed thee in the belly (womb) I knew thee, and before thou camest forth (were born) out of the womb I sanctified thee (set you apart) and I ordained thee a prophet (servant of the Lord) unto the nations." - Jeremiah 1:5

Please remember that **this is true of you too**! **You are a child of destiny**! Pray this simple prayer of commitment with me:

"Dear Lord, help me to see myself as You see me. Help me to know Your purpose and calling for my life! Come and dwell in me, and direct me from within. Amen."

This is one key to successful living!

KEY 2 **THINKING CONTROLS BEING**

Did you know that well-ordered thinking controls well-being? It is possible to control your life with a positive sense of expectancy, purpose and vitality. This is the happy norm for your life. Some may see this as naive and wishful thinking. They who do, live far below their level of potential. Because the level of their expectation is so low, the quality of life they experience will remain substandard. This was the meaning of John's salutation when he prayed:

"Beloved, I wish above all things that thou mayest prosper and be in good health, even as thy soul (psuche) prospereth." - 3 John 2

The Greek word *psuche*, is translated here as "soul". It literally refers to your mind. English words such as psychology, psychiatry and psychometrics are derived from it. In one simple statement, John, the Apostle, taught us an entire university course on Human Psychology and Modern Life. He declared that your well-being is directly related to your attitude of heart and mind!

It is a scientific fact that your physical condition is largely determined by your emotional and mental expectations. It is also true that your emotional responses are regulated by the way you think. Your thinking regulates your feelings, and this in turn governs your health and affects your well-being. When you think painful or unpleasant thoughts, it results in painful or unpleasant emotions.

I once met a man who was a perfect example of the above. He had suffered severe losses. His wife died, his business went into bankruptcy, his "fair-weather" friends abandoned him and his peers criticized him bitterly. Despite this, I found him indomitable. He was full of energy and eagerly planning the future. His face reflected peace and confidence. It was a genuine pleasure to be in his presence. When asked how he managed to sustain such a healthy outlook on life, he replied:

"I never worry! God is sovereign! It is He who gives and He who takes away. I have complete trust in Him. I reject all self-pity. I hold no grudges. I resist all painful memories and thoughts. But most importantly, I refuse to worry! I trust in my Lord implicitly and I don't worry!"

I had come to his home to encourage him, but it was I who was enriched by his faith! I had learned a valuable lesson, and determined to follow his example.

If you evaluate all the concerns which plague you on a daily basis, you will discover some startling statistics. Of all the things a person worries about, the following statistics are true:

- 40% will never happen!
- 30% is in the past and cannot be changed!
- 12% is petty and insignificant!
- 10% is related to health!
- 8% is based on reality!

Ninety-two percent of all mental and emotional energy is expended on unnecessary worry! That is alarming indeed. What a futile waste of time and energy. After a moment of thoughtful consideration, answer this thought-provoking question: "How productive could you become if this energy could be channelled into more purposeful areas of your life?"

Philippians 4:6-9 is filled with positive direction. The Apostle Paul encourages us with these words:

> *"Don't worry over anything whatever; tell God every detail of your needs in earnest and thankful prayer, and the peace of God, which transcends human understanding, will keep constant guard over your hearts and minds as they rest in Jesus Christ ... fix your mind on whatever is true and honourable and just and pure and lovely and praise-worthy ... and you will find that the God of peace will be with you." (Paraphrased)*

Four essentials stand out predominantly, and they are imperative if peace of heart and mind is to be achieved!

1. DO NOT WORRY ABOUT ANYTHING, EVER!

The Greek text uses three negatives in one sentence to emphasize this statement. "Don't never worry about nothing!" This may be poor English, but it is faultless Greek and great psychology! No exceptions are permitted. Worry is not an alternative to confidence in God. What worry declares, is that God is not big enough to handle this one. Herein lies the sin of unbelief.

2. TELL GOD EVERY DETAIL OF YOUR NEEDS!

With prayer, supplication and thanksgiving, present your concerns to God. This is the only acceptable alternative to worry. Tell it to Jesus. And how are we instructed to do this? With **prayer, supplication** and **thanksgiving.** Underscore this in your thinking: one-third of your prayer time should be spent in the giving of thanks! The most therapeutic process known to mankind is gratitude. This is the reason for the scriptural admonition : *"But godliness with contentment is great gain."* - 1 Timothy 6:6, and

> *"In every thing give thanks (in every circumstance): for this is the will of God in Christ Jesus concerning you (this is God's will for you)."*
> *- 1 Thessalonians 5:18*

3. FIX YOUR MIND UPON THE GOOD !

God is sovereign and it is He who controls the final outcome of your life. However, it is your responsibility to control your thinking process. Every person is accountable for what he or she thinks about. Man is not an emotional or mental puppet which dances on the strings of random happenings. It is I alone who will choose what I will think about. This is the reason for Paul's admonition:

> *"Finally, brethren, whatsoever things are true ... honest ... just ... pure ... lovely ... of good report; if there be any virtue ... praise,* **think on these things.**" *- Philippians 4:8*

King David clearly understood this dynamic and asked God for help to control his thought-life. Listen to his prayer as recorded in Psalm 139:23-24:

> *"Search me, O God, and know my heart: try me, and know my thoughts: And see if there be any wicked way in me, and lead me in the way everlasting."*

4. YOUR PEACE SHALL BE ESTABLISHED !

The peace that the world is looking for today, is well within reach. It is a direct result of obedience to the instructions given by Jesus, the Prince of Peace. Where does one start? What does one do to bring about happiness and well-being in life? Perhaps the place to start would be to sing this old hymn and put its philosophy of life into practice. *Count Your Blessings* has been a source of encouragement to countless people. The copyright is held by Lawrence Wright Music Co Ltd.

COUNT YOUR MANY BLESSINGS

When upon life's billows
you are tempest tossed,
When you are discouraged,
thinking all is lost,

Count your many blessings,
name them one by one,
And it will surprise you
what the Lord hath done.

Are you ever burdened
with a load of care?
Does the cross seem heavy
you are called to bear?
Count your many blessings,
every doubt will fly,
And you will keep singing
as the days go by.

So, amid the conflict,
whether great or small,
Do not be disheartened,
God is over all;
Count your many blessings,
angels will attend,
Help and comfort give you
to your journey's end.

Count your many blessings,
name them one by one;
Count your many blessings,
see what God hath done!
Count your many blessings,
name them one by one;
And it will surprise you
what the Lord hath done!

The admonition of this old hymn can be reduced to one simple formula:

Thinking   = Emotions
Emotions = Being

This is one key to successful living!

KEY 3   THE END RESULT

Most people can be divided into three general classes. There are those who make things happen, those who watch things happen, and those who say, "Huh? What just happened??" As a matter of interest, you too fall into one of these categories! Let us briefly analyse each group.

1. THE "HUH, WHAT JUST HAPPENED ?" GROUP

These are they who see the world around them, but have little comprehension as to what is going on. They are in a state of passive existence, sitting in inactivity and watching the world go by. They show little more initiative than an organic carrot. Their form of excitement is to watch grass grow. The theme song for this group goes something like this:

> Two, four, six, eight,
> We sit around
> and vegetate!

These poor people are merely existing as opposed to living. The only contribution they make to the world in which they live, is the consumption of the National Growth Product. Such a person rides on the tide of circumstance, waiting for the "lucky break", for that "Knight in shining armour" to gallop past on his steed and sweep the damsel off her feet, to ride off into the setting sun, there to live happily ever after.

Such a person does not understand that this occurs only in a fairyland fantasy. Their world of reality is therefore limited to random circumstance and wishful thinking. In endless futility, they wait for that day when their "boat comes in", when their "rich uncle dies", when the TV show host knocks on the front door with a "million dollar cheque" or when they "win the lottery". How sad! With all the creative power that is theirs, they show no more motivation than a cultured mushroom. It is unlikely that this person will ever achieve his hopes or realize his desires. Do you belong to the " Huh, what just happened?" group?

2. THE "WOW, LOOK AT IT GO" GROUP

These are they who watch it all happen. They grasp the dynamics of life and appreciate its process. There is a genuine understanding of cause and effect relationships. These are people who are perceptive and observant but neglect the motivation to act upon what they know to be right. This person is an armchair observer, rather than a participant. Such a person gives credibility to the term, *Couch Potato!* They are far beyond the "Huh, what just happened?" group in their understanding of reality, but because they do not act upon the knowledge they have, thy differ little. This person is like the man who sits on a cactus, knowing full well the cause for the discomfort, but being reluctant to move off! Their *end result* is the same. He knows the causes for his circumstances, and the steps that must be taken to correct them, but does nothing about it. Such a person is in serious danger. This is the import of James 4:17:

"Whoever knows what is right to do and fails to do it, for him it is sin."
(Paraphrased)

The majority of church-goers fall into this category. Modern Christianity can be compared to a sports event like football, rugby or soccer. In this scenario we have some twenty men running, kicking, throwing, pushing and struggling to make a score; perspiring, exhausted and desperately needing rest. All the while the sports arena is filled with eighty thousand spectators, shaking their fists, shouting their opinion and desperately needing exercise.

One armchair sports enthusiast confessed his sedentary life style. "I used to watch the PGA (Professional Golfing Association) tournaments on TV a lot, but my doctor said I was not getting enough exercise. So now I watch football, soccer, rugby and hockey." It is unlikely that this decision will improve his shape. Man was created with feet, not roots. God's intent was that man be mobile. Do you belong to the "Wow, look at it go!" group? If you do, the wise and prudent thing to do, is to get moving!

3. THE "HERE, LET ME DO IT" GROUP

These are the people who make things happen! They are the **doers,** the **trend-setters**. Life to them is more than a game of chance. It is filled with grand design and purpose. It is a work of art which reflects bold and deliberate strokes. Such a person is never preoccupied with petty hurts. He harbours no bitterness. He accepts constructive criticism and disregards the malicious. Every negative emotion is replaced with positive expectation. He is a happy person who sees the good before analysing the bad. He thinks constructively and purposefully. He seldom talks about "good luck" or the "lucky break." Personal inconvenience is disregarded. He talks about ideas, plans, goals and not about other people. These are they who recognize that all the qualities and powers of God are within them. They have discovered the reality of Genesis 1:26 and have taken charge of their lives.

"God said, Let us make man in our image ... and let them have dominion ..."

Because of this, they are able to establish realistic goals, direct their efforts towards them, and achieve them. The end results are dramatically different. All the qualities of God are wrapped in human flesh. Your flesh. As weak as your efforts may be, you are none the less created in His image and empowered by His strength. If you lack self-confidence, then move in faith. No one succeeds by the strength of personal prowess. *"The steps of a good man are ordered by the Lord."* - *Psalm 37:23*

Answer these five thought-provoking questions and place a check mark in the appropriate column:

1. With which group do you have most in common?   a)... b)... c)...

2. Into which group would others place you?   a)... b)... c)...

3. To which group do most of your friends belong?   a)... b)... c)...

4. By which group would you like to be accepted?   a)... b)... c)...

5. For today, with which group will you identify?   a)... b)... c)...

a) The "Huh,What Just Happened?" Group.
b) The "Wow, Look At It Go!" Group.
c) The "Here, Let Me Do It!" Group.

This is one key to successful living!

KEY 4   SEVEN DISEASES OF THE SOUL

Health-care is big business. More money is spent on health-care and health-care related items than on national defence. People are preoccupied with their physical aches and pains and the medicine prescribed yearly measures in the hundreds of tons (kilograms). A story is told about a hypochondriac who took so many pills that she was eventually saturated with medicine. Her doctor was quite disturbed. Each time she sneezed, all the patients in his waiting room were cured!

Physical sickness is a national preoccupation. However, diseases of the attitude are to be dreaded more than any terminal illness. The diseased body may be healed or it can find sweet relief in death, but diseases of the soul produce a living death, an enduring agony of the heart and mind that seems interminable! It poisons every moment of every day with gnawing hopelessness. The fortunate news is that diseases of the attitude can be identified and cured.

Here is a record of seven dreaded diseases of the soul and their symptoms. They are to be feared more than terminal illness. Check your attitude against this list, to see if you have been infected.

1. NESCIENCE

The word nescience means "to lack in knowledge; ignorance." Those who lack the interest or openness to examine the facts, choose to live in darkness. They will lack in knowledge. Yet knowledge is imperative in making wise choices. The telling catch-phrases go something like this: "If I had only known what an inflexible old goat he was, I would never have married him. If I had known that the stock market would decline so sharply, I wouldn't have lost my shirt. If I had known that the teacher was going to spring a test on the class, I would have studied. If I had known that my fuel tank was empty, I wouldn't have gone on the freeway!" Such statements have been repeated many times by many people.

Choices are rational decisions based on knowledge. Every choice you make is based on the information you have. If the information is lacking or erroneous, the choices will be faulty. This is clearly illustrated by our government. Every nation has a Bureau of Disinformation. Operating under a variety of names, the Bureau's main function is to disseminate misinformation. There is a good reason for this. Does any country want the enemy to have a working knowledge of its secret codes, stock piles, plans, procedures or capabilities? This would be tantamount to suicide. Therefore facts are classified or "leaked out" as misinformation. Anyone acting upon misinformation is certain to make wrong choices.

The prophets Isaiah and Hosea established the danger of ignorance when they declared:

"Therefore my people are gone into captivity, because they have no knowledge: and their honourable men are famished, and their multitudes dried up with thirst." - Isaiah 5:13

"My people are destroyed for lack of knowledge." - Hosea 4:6

The story is told of a Sunday School teacher who wrote her pastor a letter, sharing her concern for the lack of spiritual awareness in the church. She cited an incident where she was teaching her class on Joshua and the walls of Jericho. "Johnny, tell me," she asked, "who knocked down the walls of Jericho?" "I didn't do it, honest," he protested. The Pastor answered the teacher's letter and offered his condolences. "I have known Johnny and his parents a long time. If he said he didn't do it, then I must believe him, but I will take it up with the Church Board to see what can be done about it." At the Board Meeting much time was dedicated to Johnny and the wall of Jericho. One member implied that neighbourhood kids may have vandalized it. Another suggested that the wind may have blown it down. A third volunteered that it probably was old and needed replacement. The Board Chairman became impatient with all the time that was wasted in discussing such a minor incident and offered this solution. "Look, it couldn't cost that much money. Let's take it out of the church funds and replace the confounded thing."

The enemy uses ignorance as his primary weapon. Any action based upon misinformation is certain of failure. In a similar way, the enemy of the soul has a vested interest in your ignorance. If he can keep you from discovering who you really are in Christ Jesus and the victory and authority Jesus won for you at Calvary, then your marginal and substandard existence is guaranteed. This was the import of Jesus' statement when He taught:

> "Ye shall know the truth, and the truth shall make you free." - John 8:32

2. INDIFFERENCE

A deacon of a church was asked for his opinion. "Tell me, Deacon Jones," asked the pastor, "what do you think is the churches greatest blight? Is it ignorance or indifference?" After a short moment, he replied, "Well I don't know, and frankly, I couldn't care." In his case, it was both!

Indifference is a curse.

Indifferent people are uninvolved people. These individuals contribute little to those around them. They are self-centred and self-accommodating. Such an attitude creates an isolation from the very people and experiences which could enrich them. They deny themselves the satisfaction derived from befriending others. They recluse into a narrow world of private interests. If this describes your attitude, I encourage you to come out of your shell! Improve the world around you by making a meaningful contribution to it. Be something more than just another pretty face.

3. INDECISION

Mankind instinctively pursues that which is pleasurable and carefully avoids the unpleasant. Conflict arises when a person finds himself drawn or repelled by choices of equal consequences. "I hate my boss and would quit in a moment, but where would I find another job? I'd like to go back to school but I would have to sell my car. I'd leave my husband in an instant, but how would I support myself and the children?"

Such attitudes are frequently voiced. People who are indecisive vacillate between, "Yes, I will do it now," and "No, I'd better stay and tolerate it longer." The tendency is to do nothing! They hesitate in making any life-changing choices, and in so doing, they simply endure the unpleasantness and hate every moment of it. Such conflicts are highly disruptive and can cause reactions such as functional nervous disorders, neurosis, hysterical illness and psychosomatic disorders.

Examine all your options. There are alternatives available to you other than staying or leaving. List the ways whereby you can change your circumstances. Then arrange them in order, starting with the least traumatic "earth shattering choice". Determine to do something about them, then get started. Move forward until results are found. One thing is certain, you do not have to endure life. You must enjoy it!

Do not be afraid to make a choice and live by it. There are times when a poor choice is better than no choice at all. In flying from A to B, an airliner makes many mid-course corrections. It does not mean that the plane is off course, simply because it has to circumvent a few thunderstorms. It is on its way to its destination according to flight plans and will arrive there. If your current course of action encounters strong head-winds, don't give up. Should a storm confront you, you can always find a way around it.

4. WORRY OR ANXIETY

Anxiety disables more people than all other health problems combined. Worry is an emotional tension. It is characterized by apprehension, fearfulness, mental pain and numerous physical reactions. The root meaning of the word worry is to strangle; to harass by tearing, snapping, biting, especially at the throat. Worry is tormenting. It afflicts with mental distress and results in preoccupying concerns. Worry is constricting and suffocating! It is for this reason that Philippians 4:6-7 warns:

> *"Don't you never worry for nothing, nohow, (this is a literal transla-tion from the Greek) but in everything by prayer and supplication ... let your requests be made known unto God! And the peace of God, which passes all understanding, shall keep your hearts and minds through Christ Jesus."*

Abandon your worries to God! You can entrust all your concerns to Him. He has both the resources and the interest to care for you. Give place to encouragement! Expect the best and see it come to pass.

5. OVER-CAUTIOUSNESS

It is impossible to go on to anything new without leaving the old behind. You cannot read a new book without laying the old one aside. A family cannot live in a new home without vacating the former. An employee cannot take a new job without terminating the previous employment. You cannot eat in a new restaurant without being absent from your customary place. The examples are many. In spite of this obvious fact, there is a cautiousness to try something new.

The old offers a form of security. Familiarity extends a measure of acceptance, assurance and confidence. The new carries with it uncertainty, inconvenience and discomfort. The pioneering experience is never without its uncertainties and traumas. The dividends however, far outweigh the difficulties. Those who fear uncertainty, will carefully avoid anything that may produce it. As a result, they seldom venture out into the new, but rather become quite comfortable in their reclusive state.

Be bold! Be strong! The Lord your God is with you! Don't be afraid of failure. If you fail in 80% of all you attempt, you are still 20 times ahead of the person who has never tried anything. A rock and a corpse have one thing in common: **they never fail!** When you see a person who has failed, understand that it was someone who had tried.

6. PESSIMISM

An optimist is a man who grabs his fishing-rod when he discovers that his basement has been flooded with water. While the optimist is turning on the lights to dispel the darkness, the pessimist blows out the candle to see how dark it is. The very nature of expectation is self-fulfilling, because it is always searching for evidence to verify its conviction. Positive expectation is therefore imperative to well-being.

Twixt the optimist and the pessimist,
the difference is very droll:
The optimist sees the doughnut,
while the pessimist sees the hole!

The young church at Philippi needed encouragement. We all need to heed the admonition which the Apostle Paul gave the early Christians:

"Finally, brethren,
whatsoever things are true,
whatsoever things are honest,
whatsoever things are just,
whatsoever things are pure,

whatsoever things are lovely,
whatsoever things are of good report;
if there be any virtue, and if there
be any praise,
think on these things." *- Philippians 4:8*

7. IMPATIENCE

"For everything there is a time," said Solomon. Everything on earth functions within a time frame. Every farmer knows that a kernel of grain takes 90 days to grow to maturity. Impatience can be illustrated by the farmer who plants his seed in the morning, and uncovers them that evening to see if they have germinated. This he continues every morning and evening, and after a month is distressed because no growth has occurred. A frustrated lady, who was stressed beyond her limits, entreated the Lord for patience. "Dear Lord," she prayed, "give me patience, and give it to me right now!" Be patient! Let patience have her perfect work in your life. Leave it alone and let it be. Listen to Paul's testimony concerning Abraham:

"For when God made promises to Abraham, because he could swear
by no greater, he sware by himself, Saying surely blessing I will bless
thee, and multiplying I will multiply thee. And so, after he had
patiently endured, *he obtained the promise ... Wherein God, willing*
more abundantly to shew unto the heirs of promise, the immutability
of his counsel ... in which it was impossible for God to lie, we might
have a **strong consolation,** *who have fled for refuge to lay hold upon*
the hope set before us." - Hebrews 6:13-18

Each disease of the soul can be cured by following the corrective procedures as prescribed by the Great Physician:

"If my people, which are called by my name, shall humble themselves,
and pray, and seek my face, and turn from their wicked ways; then
will I hear from heaven, and will forgive their sin, and will heal their
land." - 2 Chronicles 7:14

This is one key to successful living!

KEY 5   HOW TO STAY WELL AND BE HAPPY

If you are sick and tired of being sick and tired, use this key to unlock the door to happiness and well-being. The key is guaranteed to work, but it must be used if it is to be effective. If you could discover a formula that would make you wealthy and ensure your happiness and well-being, would you try it? If there was the remotest chance that it might work, would you try it? Some may say, "No." If not, then "Why Not?" Does anyone enjoy a sub-standard existence? Have we become so accepting of deficiency that it has become a norm? Have we learned to expect nothing more out of life than mediocrity? Your expectation becomes your realization! If this is true of you, then this adage is for you:

Blessed is he who expects nothing, for he shall never be disappointed!

Expectation is self-fulfilling. It is prophetic in the sense that expectation is a cause which is always looking for confirmation. It is a certainty that a man will never receive anything more from life than what he expects. Expect nothing, receive nothing! Anticipate the best, and you will find the good.

There are many who desire more out of life than what they have been getting. They want to be happy and well. They long to wake up in the morning feeling refreshed and excited about their day. They yearn for happy relationships with their family, friends and peers. They would like to retire for the evening knowing that their day was fulfilling, and with a sense of expectation that tomorrow would be the same. Unrealistic? No! A thousand times NO! This is not a vain delusion. Achieving fulfilment in life must be the expected norm for each person. If this is your desire, then the following formula can make it a reality:

"A cheerful heart is good medicine, but a crushed spirit dries up the bones." - Proverbs 17:22 (New International Version)

Emotions and attitudes have a profound affect on your physical condition and personal demeanour. Here is how it works. The neurological and psychological dynamics of the brain are divided into two systems: the central nervous system (CNS), consisting of the brain and the spinal cord, and the peripheral nervous system (PNS), which are the nerve fibres. Two processes occur here: the somatic, conscious functions (SF) and the autonomic, automatic functions (AF).

CNS + PNS = SF + AF

A home computer operates in much the same way. It consists of two systems: the program disk, which is a constant automatic function regulating a particular program, and the data disk, into which information is fed. The human brain contains over 100 billion neurons, each having the sophistication and the capacity of a home computer. God placed a "flesh and blood" computer in man's cranium which outstrips man's finest invention! This is mind-staggering but true.

1. THE SOMATIC NERVOUS SYSTEM

The somatic nervous system governs consciousness. This includes perception, cognition and awareness. This is the system through which we relate to the outside world of reality. Incoming stimuli reach the mind via sensory perception. We record all that we see, hear, taste, smell and touch. This information is then identified, analysed, evaluated, catalogued and stored. When a response is required, the information is retrieved. Incoming stimuli are compared with all data stored, and evaluated against the backdrop of current circumstances. After exploring all options and contingencies, a choice is made and a course of action is determined. Behaviour is predicated upon the information received. This is the reason for the modern-day computer adage:

Garbage in, garbage out !

The information which you accept, in a very real way determines your behaviour. The following example illustrates this fact. Should you encounter a lion on your evening stroll, your accumulated knowledge warns you that you are in immanent danger. Evasive action is not only appropriate and prudent but also very urgent! You had better **exit**, stage right or left, **split**! The dynamics are not difficult to understand. I see a lion and my mind computes immanent danger. Adrenalin is released into my system, urgent messages are dispatched to every nerve of my being, and I **split** ! The Psalmist, David, knew the importance of this concept. He understood how behaviour is determined by the thought-processes. This is the reason he penned these words:

"Thy word have I hid in mine heart, that I might not sin against thee."
- Psalm 119:11

What he was saying was: the very concepts I store in my mind, are those notions which will control all my behaviour. This holds true whether that behaviour is sinful or righteous.

2. THE AUTONOMIC NERVOUS SYSTEM

The autonomic nervous system (ANS) regulates visceral and glandular responses. It is totally automatic. No one needs to be reminded to wind the heart, change the filters in the kidneys, start the digestive processes after a meal, or recharge the cadmium batteries for the mental word processor. No one has ever died from "Non-memorable-respiratory-itus", that is, forgetting to breathe. All bodily functions operate automatically. There are other responses that the ANS control. This is especially evident in emergency situations. It initiates wide-spread and profound body changes including the discharge of adrenalin into the blood stream, accelerated heart beat, dilations of the bronchiole, elevation of blood pressure, increase in white blood count and induction of coagulants into the blood stream.

We can readily see how beneficial this is. Let us suppose that you meet a hungry lion while on your evening walk. Your autonomic nervous system would automatically take over all functions. Adrenalin would be pumped into your system increasing alertness, perception, reflexes and strength. Your heart would accelerate, increasing energy for flight. Digestion would stop, diverting all power to the limbs. Air intake would increase providing a greater supply of oxygen. The white blood count would increase. This would aid in killing any infection the body might sustain. Increased coagulants in the blood stream would lessen haemorrhaging. This and much more occur without thought, instantaneously, and automatically. Your entire being would be placed on alert, and you would enter a "flight or fight mode". In the case of the lion, I assure you it would be flight! Each time a person encounters a threatening situation, all this happens automatically. Amazing! How grand are these bodies that we live in, that they should protect and care for themselves automatically.

There is another interesting feature about the automatic nervous system. The ANS is incapable of discerning the difference between a real lion and an imaginary one! Should you imagine the same threatening lion, your body will go into the same preparedness and defensive posture. We all have been frightened into paralysis by something we later discovered to be insignificant. Think of the alarming implications. Every time you think of that painful divorce, you go through the same reactions as though you were standing before the judge at that present moment. Every time you feel bitterness or hate towards some rival, you suffer the same stress as though you are presently locked in the conflict. Every time you remember something unpleasant of the past, imagine your inadequacies, envision your failures, or hear the demeaning voices of the past, your autonomic nervous system prepares your body for **fight or flight**! This places tremendous stress on your system. It is no wonder that our bodies struggle under the stress, our minds weary under the strain, and our faces age before the mirror. It is amazing that our bodies function at all when we consider the poisonous attitudes, toxic emotions and destructive thoughts we harbour.

The prophet, Jeremiah, lamented for his people who were distraught and hurting. They could find no place where they could gain peace or healing or happiness or well-being. Their attempts at finding healing were futile. Evidently they were looking for it in the wrong places.

"Go up into Gilead (the place of God's protection), and take balm (receive healing), O virgin, the daughter of Egypt (all those who are hurting): in vain shalt thou use many medicines, for thou shalt not be cured (for all your medical contrivances can affect no healing)." - Jeremiah 46:11

Those who desire peace, healing, happiness and well-being, are encouraged to go to God. It is He who created the body. He knows how He divided the somatic nervous system from the autonomic nervous system, and how each functions. He provided a book of instructions (the Bible) which tells us how to operate our bodies to full capacity and with optimum efficiency. It is He who tells us how to live happily and how to possess well-being. It may be that you have tried every other formula. Why not try this one:

"A happy spirit is like a medicine to the bones ..." - Proverbs 17:22 (Paraphrased)

People who have a happy spirit do not imagine painful experiences. They do not harbour caustic attitudes or think harmful thoughts. They are not preoccupied with bitter memories. They do not immerse themselves in their fears, failures or uncertainties. They are not negative, critical or judgmental. People who have a happy spirit refuse to entertain damaging expectations. Happy-spirited people know their God. For these reasons they are people who have found peace, healing and well- being.

I, for one, am determined to live this way to the best of my ability! Will you join me? Make this confession with me:

"Lord, this day I shall be obedient to your precepts. I shall expect your blessing. I will be a **happy-spirited** person. By your enabling power I shall live victoriously. This is my finest hour."

This is one key to successful living!

KEY 6   LUCKY OR JINXED?

How lucky are you? Have you ever won anything? Does everything you touch turn to gold? Do you have a green thumb? Are you lucky or are you like the "born-loser" who complained that if he didn't have bad luck, he would have no luck at all. Which is true of you? Are you a *Lucky Louie* or a *Jinxed Josephine*? Perhaps you are neither. Possibly you are blessed of God!

A sixteen year old boy came to my office under court order. He was arrested for breaking in and entering. His only theft was ladies under-garments. Within fifteen minutes it became evident that his crime was only a symptom of a much deeper problem. He tripped over a carpet as he entered the office and grunted, "I guess I have two left feet." During the session he dropped a pen to the floor and said, "I was born with ten thumbs." He knocked a book off the desk and sighed, "Clumsy me." He was very obese and referred to himself as "Jumbo Buffo", an uncomplimentary term meaning "huge buffalo". He had no friends and no recognition. His main grievance was that he succeeded at nothing. In describing his encounter with the law he said, "I am the most unlucky person on the whole earth. I've got to be jinxed."

The lad was neither unlucky nor jinxed. He was blessed of God! This fact, however, was never made clear to him. He was never told that he

was wanted, loved or important. No one had ever told him that God
formed him exactly as He wished him to be, and that He loved him just
as he was. No one ever embraced him with assuring approval. He did
not know that he was special. He never heard the story of the prophet
Jeremiah who had similar fears and feelings, and how God encouraged
him:

> *"Then the word of the Lord came unto me, saying, Before I formed
> thee in the belly, I knew thee; and before thou camest forth out of the
> womb I sanctified thee, and I ordained thee a prophet unto the
> nations." - Jeremiah 1:4-5*

He never received words of approval such as: "Son, you did well! I'm
proud of you! You are important to me." He was never asked for his
opinion. He was talked at and to, but seldom with. He was scorned,
belittled and rebuked. His parents constantly compared him with his
elder brother who was a high achiever and respected by his peers. His
teacher called him a dummy. He was denigrated by his peers and girls
were embarrassed to be seen with him. What other conclusion could he
make? Obviously, he was a failure, just a "big, dumb, ugly slob!" Such a
harmful self-image has a direct bearing on our attitudes, emotions and
performance.

The world is governed by sovereign law. In a universe which operates
according to divine order and is governed by cause and effect
relationships in every infinite detail, there is no such thing as luck,
random chance, misfortune or coincidence. The contrary is true. Every
person is the unique product of God's genius, created unto good works.
God's final product is never an embarrassment to Him. He does not
specialize in creating rubbish. This is the import of the admonition given
to the Christians at Ephesis:

> *"For we are his workmanship, created in Christ Jesus unto good
> works, which God hath before ordained that we should walk in them."
> - Ephesians 2:10*

By analogy, the automobile is the proud workmanship of the manufacturing company. It is engineered for pleasure, comfort and safe driving. If the car was manufactured according to specifications and is driven within the framework of its limitations, every goal will be achieved. The key is to drive the car according to manufacturer's specifications. The car was not designed to pull a plough or to haul three cords of firewood. It was never intended to be an off-road vehicle. It was not engineered to fly beneath radar detection at hypersonic speeds. It must have the recommended amounts of coolant, oil, air and fuel. It must be driven somewhere between the centre line of the road and the ditch. It is **bad luck** to park your new convertible near a barn yard hen-house. It is a certainty that you will be most **unlucky** if you drive your car without oil or coolant. You will be permanently **jinxed** should you wander into the lane of oncoming traffic. Is this bad luck or a matter of carelessness? What is claimed as **bad luck**, is often an excuse for poor judgement and irresponsible behaviour. In most instances misfortune is nothing more than the consequence of a deviation. When a person violates an established law or principle, the results can be most unpleasant:

Unlucky ... unfortunate ... jinxed

The lad in question was charged with a serious violation, but it was not his "panty escapades" which inflicted the greatest damage to his character. His violation was his destructive, demeaning self-image. Such harmful concepts are sure to work havoc in a person's life. He was convinced that he was clumsy, big, ugly, "unlike" and jinxed to failure. Because of this expectation, he unconsciously, yet deliberately, put himself in situations which would prove his assessment accurate. Ancient Job alluded to the power of self-concept when he confessed:

"For the thing which I greatly feared is come upon me, and that which I was afraid of is come unto me." - Job 3:25

In the passage of a few months, this young man's image of himself changed, and consequently also his attitude, behaviour and performance. His "panty capers" ceased and so did his excessive eating.

Oral and sexual pleasures gave way to meaningful relationships and activities. He is an adult today, happily married and successfully employed.

Gary Player, the well known participant of the PGA (Professional Golf Association), was interviewed by a reporter after one of his victories. "Would you comment on that classic *lucky* shot which won you the tournament?" the reporter asked. After several interesting comments about the course, the ball positioning and weather conditions, Mr Player added, "I have noticed that the more I practice, the *luckier* I get!" By his own admission, Thomas Jefferson was a great believer in luck. "I'm a great believer in luck," he said, "and I find that the harder I work, the more I have of it!" In most cases, it takes twenty years to become an overnight success. Only a failure believes that success is a matter of luck. It would do us all well to remember that:

Luck is the idol of the idle!

Here are some helpful directives which can make you serendipity lucky.

1. ACKNOWLEDGE THE LAWS OF DIVINE ORDER

God alone is in charge of the cause and effect relationships which govern the universe. Obey His principles and leave the outcome to Him. Samuel charged King Saul that "... *to obey is better than sacrifice, and to hearken than the fat of rams.*" - 1 Samuel 15:22. Listen to David's dying instruction to his son Solomon:

> "*I go the way of all the earth: be thou strong therefore, and shew thyself a man; And keep the charge of the* **Lord** *thy God, to walk in his ways, to keep his statutes, and his commandments, and his judgments, and his testimonies, as it is written in the law of Moses, that thou mayest prosper in all that thou doest, and whithersoever thou turnest thyself.*"
> *- 1 Kings 2:2-3*

2. RECOGNIZE YOUR UNIQUE PURPOSE

There is no other person in the universe just like you. God made you as a limited edition of **one**, and He threw the mould away upon your completion. No other person can fill your purpose. Do you comprehend the far-reaching implications? If you fail to function as God has ordained, the world will be forever disadvantaged, because it will lack your contribution. Don't rob others of the blessing which you could be to them.

3. FUNCTION ACCORDING TO YOUR CALLING

You have both ability and calling. Although you may succeed through natural talent alone, it is the calling of God that carries with it His anointing. Herein lies genuine prosperity. Natural ability plays a secondary role in success.

"Each one should use whatever gift he has received to serve others, faithfully administering God's grace in its various forms. If anyone speaks, he should do it as one speaking the very words of God. If anyone serves, he should do it with the strength God provides, so that in all things God may be praised through Jesus Christ." - 1 Peter 4:10-11 (New International Version)

4. ENVISION LOFTY GOALS

If a project is within your reach, it doesn't need God's help. You can achieve it on your own. If your goals are beyond your limitations, you will need His guidance and strength to reach them. Don't limit God with pallid expectations and paltry projects. Without faith it is impossible to please Him. Make a personal study of Hebrews chapter eleven and discover the great exploits which were accomplished through faith. These were accomplished by ordinary men and women who trusted in their unlimited God.

5. KEEP YOUR FOCUS ON THE END RESULTS

Never become discouraged with the lack of progress. Thomas A Edison had more than one thousand failures before he invented the light bulb. The key to his success is found in his reply to a reporter: "Genius is one percent inspiration and ninety-nine percent perspiration." Your hands may be dirty, but your job is not yet finished. Patiently wait for the end result. Success must never be viewed as an event, but rather as a process. A bumper sticker on a car explained it well: " **Christians aren't perfect, they are in the process of becoming that way!**"

6. BE ALERT, PERCEPTIVE AND PURSUING

Be sharp! Look sharp! Carry yourself with confidence. If anyone can walk with a bounce in his step, have a whistle on his lips and a smile on his face, it is the child of God. We have the mind of Christ, we possess the peace of God which passes understanding, and our steps are directed by God. God will grant you the ability to perform beyond your natural talents and personal acumen. This was Job's conclusion when he declared:

"... *there is a spirit in man: and the inspiration of the Almighty giveth them understanding.*" - *Job 32:8*

7. DON'T BECOME DISCOURAGED

Every project has its reversals. Each undertaking is fraught with the tedious, the mundane and the distasteful. If you become preoccupied with the unpleasant present, you will fail to achieve your future goals. President Grover Cleveland made the following observation:

"Unswerving loyalty to duty, constant devotion to truth, and a clear conscience, will overcome every discouragement and will surely lead to usefulness and high achievement."

8. BE HONEST WITH YOURSELF

It is not a sign of weakness to admit to error. Failing does not make you a failure. You are not deficient because you ask for help. You are not lacking simply because you seek counsel. The contrary is true. Listen to the words of Solomon, the wisest man of all times:

"The way of a fool is right in his own eyes: but he that hearkeneth unto counsel is wise." - *Proverbs 12:15*

9. ACCEPT YOURSELF WHERE YOU ARE AT

Carefully avoid self-condemnation. There is no greater obstacle to personal fulfilment than the inferiority complex. Discouragement and a lack of self-confidence breed mundane mediocrity. You must avoid self-abasement. You may not be where you want to be, but be grateful that you are not where you used to be.

"There is therefore now no condemnation to them which are in Christ Jesus, who walk not after the flesh, but after the Spirit." - *Romans 8:1*

10. ENJOY GOD'S BLESSING

All God's creatures pursue the purpose for which they were created - to **enjoy life!** All God's creatures relish life, except mankind. An outside observer would conclude that most men tolerate life. Life was not intended to be endured like a painful tooth ache or avoided like a root canal treatment. Life was designed to be enjoyed. Lord, grant us a sense of humour and give us the gift of laughter. Smite us with happiness, and may we never recover!

Call it lucky if you insist, but remember that success, happiness and well-being are consequences of divine order and of human effort. A successful life is not fortuitous serendipity - it is an achievement. In other words, you are **blessed of God.**

This is one key to successful living!

KEY 7   TROUBLE CAN BE A FRIEND

Trouble is rarely viewed as beneficial. It is seen as a sinister monster possessing every propensity of evil. It is perceived as the major cause of a variety of complications ranging from mental disorders to marital strife. It includes such dynamics as emotional strain, neurotic disorders, functional disturbances, interpersonal conflicts, physical reactions, dysfunctional behaviour and unhappiness.

The masochist finds pleasure in pain and seeks opportunity for it. The suffering hero gains recognition from the pain and courageously endures it. Because of the attention he receives, he frequently welcomes it. The fatalist sees unalterable hopelessness in trouble and passively accepts it. The idealist lives in a state of denial, sees only that which is beyond the pain, and thus ignores the pain. The realist knows that each adversity contains the seeds of opportunity, thus he dutifully endures the unpleasantness. He understands that every problem is limited by a sunset clause and its life span is limited! Paul, the Apostle, addressed this issue in the following passages:

> *"There hath no temptation (trial, testing, experience) taken you but such as is common to man: but God is faithful, who will not suffer you to be tempted above that ye are able; but will with the temptation also make a way to escape, that ye may be able to bear it."* -
> *1 Corinthians 10:13*

The Greek word used here is *pirasmos*. The word does not mean a solicitation to evil, but rather a trial, a testing or a trying experience. It refers to the proving of a person's fidelity under stress. In one simple word, it means **trouble!** The Latin word translated as trouble is *tribulum*. Its origin is most interesting. The *tribulum* was a threshing instrument used by early farmers. It consisted of a long handle much like a garden rake, with a flat paddle affixed to the end with a flexible leather strap. The grain was heaped on a hard surface like a flat rock, where the farmer would flail the straw with his *tribulum*. The action would break the pure kernel loose from the husk. The straw and grain were then tossed into the air, where the wind would blow away the chaff, leaving the pure grain on the threshing floor.

The lesson to be learned is clear! Trouble was never designed to harm us, but rather to remove the chaff from our lives and bring out the best in us. When we have this attitude, reversals are seen as God's opportunities!

*"We are troubled on every side, yet **not** distressed; we are perplexed but **not** in despair; persecuted, but **not** forsaken; cast down, but **not** destroyed ... for which cause we faint **not**; but though our outward man perish, yet the inward man is renewed day by day. For our light affliction, which is but for a moment, worketh for us a far more exceeding and eternal weight of glory; While we look **not** at the things which are seen, but at the things which are not seen: for the things which are seen are temporal; but the things which are not seen are eternal." - 2 Corinthians 4:8-9, 16-18*

The word **not**, is used five times in this brief passage: troubled **not** distressed; perplexed **not** in despair; persecuted **not** forsaken; cast down **not** destroyed. The sad reality is that most people place the emphasis on the phrase that proceeds the negative: **troubled, perplexed, persecuted** and **forsaken**. Such people place the **emphasis** on the wrong **syllable**! Because reality is tainted by our subjective outlook, anyone possessing a negative mind-set will find it difficult to see anything positive about life. Life to them is a "bummer". Place the emphasis where it belongs, on the right syllable. We are **not** distressed, forsaken, destroyed or in despair! "When I look back on all these worries," said Sir Winston Churchill, "I remember the story of the old man who said on his deathbed that he had had a lot of trouble in his life, most of which never happened!" Don't place the **emphasis** on the wrong **syllable**!

Several helpful facts can be learned from the above passage found in the book of Second Corinthians. They will help you to view your trying circumstance in a realistic light. You will also find some practical suggestions to help you cope. Your goal must not be to escape life's afflictions, but rather to learn how to handle them effectively!

1. YOU CAN OVERCOME YOUR PROBLEMS

No trial in life is greater than your ability to endure it. You do have the resources to be victorious in the midst of your circumstances. God is not unjust or inhumane and will not inflict such trial as is beyond your ability to handle.

2. YOUR PROBLEMS ARE NOT UNIQUE

Every trouble you may experience, is commonly experienced by others. Your station in life is not unique. Many people have experienced similar difficulties. Many have been called upon to endure far greater trials, and have done so heroically.

3. YOU ARE STRONGER THAN YOUR TROUBLES

Many people have overcome similar circumstances successfully. They were "winners" against all odds. Their testimony is that God is faithful and will not suffer you to be tested beyond your ability to bear it.

4. EVERY TROUBLE WILL COME TO AN END

Every trial has its termination. Trouble has a brief life-span! It is not unlimited. It will come to an end. Trouble may last a day, a week, a month, a year or several years, but it will end. By divine order, trouble must cease and desist! Jesus warned his disciples of a coming day of unprecedented world calamity. The narrative is found in Luke 21:8-19. He then gave them the key for survival:

"In your patience (by standing firm) possess ye your souls (you will preserve your life)." - Luke 21:19

5. TROUBLE IS A LEARNING EXPERIENCE

The process of handling stress, develops the ability to cope. Every problem carries with it the seed of its own solution. When I was a child, tying my shoe was a genuine trauma. I vividly remember the day when I tied my shoes for the first time without my mother's help. I was ecstatic! I was alone and no one was around to share my moment of victory or verify my success. But I couldn't be happier if the entire world was watching. Today, putting on my shoes is no problem. And it is not because I wear loafers. The Bible declares that suffering was a learning experience for Jesus Christ as well.

"Though he were a Son, yet learned he obedience by the things which he suffered." - Hebrews 5:8

6. TROUBLE DEVELOPS CHARACTER

The process of enduring trouble is character-building. When trials come, remember that it is "character building time!" This was the admonition of James:

"My brethren, count it all joy when you fall into various troubles; Knowing this, that the trying of your faith works patience. Let patience have her perfect work, that you may be perfect and entire, wanting nothing." - James 1:2-3

7. TROUBLE INCREASES SENSITIVITY

When you experience trials, your understanding of and empathy for others are heightened. It is said that Jesus was tested in all points as we are. He not only created us, but also became one of us and endured unspeakable agony. He knows and understands our frame, and is therefore able to succour all who are in any kind of trouble. The teaching of Hebrews 4:14-16 asserts that Jesus knows about your difficulties, and is compassionate towards your needs:

"Seeing then that we have a great high priest ... (who is) touched with the feelings of our infirmities ... Therefore come boldly unto the throne of grace, that we may obtain mercy, and find grace to help in time of need."

8. TROUBLE INCREASES SPIRITUAL INSIGHT

Dedication, sincerity and devotion are admirable qualities, but they can never increase spiritual awareness. Prayer and Bible reading are imperative, but spiritual insights are revitalized through the agency of **trouble.** It is impossible to add to the teaching of 2 Corinthians 4:16-18:

"For which cause we faint not; but though our outward man perish, yet the inward man is renewed day by day. For our **light** *affliction, which is but for a* **moment, worketh** *for us a far more exceeding and eternal weight of glory; While we look not at the things which are seen: but at the things which are not seen: for the things which are seen are temporal; but the things which are not seen are eternal (spiritual insight)."*

9. TROUBLE IS A PREPARATION FOR MINISTRY

Trouble enhances your ability to minister to others. Many are under the impression that higher learning at Bible school and seminary is the training required for ministry. God never places His premium upon ignorance. We live in a day of specialists, and he who handles God's Word must be well equipped. However, it is trouble that qualifies us for effective ministry. This message is not popular, but it is true.

"Blessed be God, even the Father of our Lord Jesus Christ, the Father of mercies, and the God of all comfort; Who comforteth us in all our tribulation, that we may be able to comfort them which are in any trouble, by the comfort wherewith we ourselves are comforted of God." - 2 Corinthians 1:3-4

10. RELIEF COMES WHEN TROUBLE IS OVER

Following each sorrow is unsorrow, that period of peace, joy and complete resolution. Never become discouraged with your trial. God is not through with you yet. You shall come through rejoicing. Trouble was never designed to destroy you, but to mould you. Only in retrospect can you see the benefits of your trials. This is the message of Hebrews 12:11-13. Note the concluding charge:

"No discipline seems pleasant at the time, but painful. Later on, however, it produces a harvest of righteousness and peace for those who have been trained by it. Therefore, strengthen your feeble arms and weak knees. Make level paths for your feet..."

She thought her world had fallen apart. After fourteen years of what seemed to be a happy marriage, her husband left her for someone else. "How am I going to care for my children? How can I possibly make the mortgage payment? After so many years out of the job market, who will hire me? Who is going to fix my car and cut the lawn or change the gasket in the dripping faucet?" Her emotions raced from self-pity to anger, from fear to determined vengeance and from depression to palled hope. She tried everything to win her husband back. She pleaded, reasoned, prayed, cried, shouted and begged. She tried the "guilt trip". Nothing worked. He was impervious to her overtures, and her greatest fear became reality.

But the story did not end there. She found it necessary to move out of her house and go to work. She lost 25 pounds (11 kg). She took a refresher course in typing and studied computer science and word processing. Today she is employed as an executive secretary in a large firm. Every morning she leaves her new home dressed in her new outfit for her new office. She radiates a confidence and happiness, and people are drawn to her. She is a joy to be with. Because of the traumas she suffered, she is able to understand those who are hurting and is able to give them wise counsel. She is faithful to her church and conducts a Bible study. "I would rather be tied to a pole in a public square and flogged with a whip, than to go through that experience again," she said. After a long pause she continued, "but I wouldn't miss one moment of that experience, for it was the main ingredient which turned me to the Lord. It made me the person that I am today. He actually did me a big favour."

Incidently, the husband came back to his wife, and acknowledged his foolishness. He submitted himself to the process of therapy, and both of them received counselling. Theirs is a true success story. It should be underscored, however, that whether he came back or not, in no way determined her new direction. She became a happy, confident person in her own right.

If you are finding difficulty bearing your trying circumstances, take courage in the words of 1 Peter 1:5-7:

"Who are kept by the power of God through faith unto salvation ...wherein ye greatly rejoice, though now for a season, if need be, ye are in heaviness through manifold temptations; that the trial of your faith, being much more precious than of gold that perisheth, though it be tried with fire, might be found unto praise and honour and glory at the appearing of Jesus Christ."

The larva struggles within its metamorphic prison, but when the butterfly emerges, everyone marvels at its beauty. No longer an earth-bound caterpillar, it wafts upward to new vistas. This is what the Lord desires for you. Let patience have her perfect work in your life. God is in the process of making you beautiful.

This is one key to successful living!

KEY 8   SURGERY OF THE SOUL

Surgery of the soul may be an unusual title to describe a change of heart and soul, but it is accurate. Furthermore, the results are far superior to any surgical procedure.

"I call them as I see them!" said one man who umpired for the little league. Most people make decisions based on the information they receive. This information is gathered through the five senses. The mind operates on the stimuli provided by our sensory perception. It is what we see, hear, smell, taste and touch that tell us what we know about the world we live in. This becomes reality to us, and forms the premise upon which every choice is made. But can we believe what we see? How accurate is sensory perception? Can we be certain that what is perceived is real? The truth is that sensory perception can be very misleading. Man is prone to misread and misunderstand. This is supported by the many times we have been mistaken, because we misinterpret the stimuli coming to us.

The story is told of a sexton (a caretaker of a church yard and cemetery) who was preparing a grave for a burial the following day. He was about to go home for the night, but as he stooped to pick up his shovel, his foot slipped and he fell into the grave. He tried to get out by jumping, by climbing the corner between the side and by pulling himself up on the sides. Every effort proved futile. He knew that a co-worker would be by early next morning, so he settled himself in one corner for a well deserved rest. At midnight the local bar closed and an inebriated patron was making his way home. To save time, he decided to take a short cut across the cemetery. He didn't see the open grave and fell into it. He tried to get out by jumping, by climbing the corner between the side and by pulling himself up on the sides. Every effort proved futile. The sexton who sat quietly watching the drama, finally spoke up, "you can't get out of here." But **he did**! With one mighty leap he was out of the grave and the cemetery at warp speed.

Have you ever had a shot of adrenalin spike your entire system into overdrive, only to discover later that what you thought you saw was only some inconsequential thing? Perception can be so inaccurate and misleading that the Bible frequently warns us against deception. With terse phrases such as: "Be not deceived. Let no man deceive you. Beware lest your mind be removed," we are cautioned to guard our minds. It has been said that seeing is believing. Magicians rely on *legere de main* (slight of hand) to make audiences believe an illusion.

What is real? It depends on who is seeing, and what is perceived. The example of four blind men describing an elephant is classic. The first, running his hands along the side of the elephant, said, "An elephant is very much like a stippled wall." The second, feeling its front leg, announced, "The elephant is the same in size and texture as a tree." Holding onto the tail, the third described the elephant as, "much like a rope used to tether a ship to the dock." The fourth, wrestling with its trunk, contended that the pachyderm, "must be a relative of the octopus."

There are two very important things to remember. First, reality (what is real and for sure) is not contingent upon **what** you see, but rather, **how** you see it. Second, reality is not the external world of objects and things which surround us, but rather the internal mind-set (disposition and attitude) from which we view. In simple terms, whether life is a **drag** or a **fantastic drama**, will be determined by your attitude.

A young college student was never satisfied. He attended schools in Canada, Florida, Colorado and Oklahoma, all for one semester only. He earned the nick-name, Tiosk, an acronym for "The International One Semester Kid." He gave a variety of reasons why he dropped out of school: "The professors are too hard. The students are biased against me. The subject matter is irrelevant. It is lonely. The weather patterns are too severe. It's like a jail." With such an attitude, it was not long before his slide downward ended in most unfortunate circumstances. He found himself languishing in a local jail cell on a misdemeanour charge.

It is frequently found that in such crisis situations, attitudes can change quickly and dramatically. Jail-house conversions have placed many men in the ministry. He realized the utter futility of his situation and determined to change his world of reality. Instead of asking his parents for more money to send him to college, he sold his possessions and enrolled in class. In a telephone conversation with his father, his voice reflected an enthusiasm which astonished his parents. "How are you getting along son?" his father asked. "Oh, just great, Dad! All the teachers like me, the guys in the dorm are fantastic and I've joined a musical group. The food is just great, there are a lot of nice girls and its only 25 below zero!" What a difference attitude can make in the world of reality! "Man must cease attributing his problems to his environment," said Albert Schweitzer, "and learn again to exercise his will!"

Paul, the Apostle, was on trial for his life. He was confined to a Roman prison cell, a cavernous hole some twenty feet (6 m) below the streets of Rome. Prisoners were lowered into their confinement with a rope. Cold, damp, overrun with vermin, and fouled with the stench of human sewage, he penned these words of hope:

"Blessed be the God and Father of our Lord Jesus Christ, who hath blessed us with all spiritual blessings in heavenly places in Christ." - *Ephesians 1:3*

In the face of the most troubling circumstances, he displayed a superb attitude. Shortly before his death, he encouraged the Christians at Philippi not to be disheartened because of his imprisonment. Two weeks later, he was executed.

Do you have any unpleasant circumstances which you would like to cut out of your life; a formidable foe you would like to hack to pieces; an obstacle you would like to slice away; a path you would like to carve through your jungle? This may all be necessary, but what you really need is a **divine surgery of the soul** ! It was for this reason that Paul charged Timothy with these words:

"Godliness with contentment is great gain." - *1 Timothy 6:6*

Pray this simple prayer:

"Lord, take away my negative, destructive attitude and grant me true contentment!"

This is one key to successful living!

KEY 9   POISON FOR THE MIND

The Food and Drug Administration (FDA) in the United States, requires that manufacturing companies display labels on all products which may be harmful for human consumption. This is done to ensure the safety of the user. It also protects the manufacturer against liability. Here are a few examples.

Draino is a solution that is designed to open clogged drains. It is reputed to unclog the most stubborn kitchen drain pipe. No damage will be done to any pipe, providing the pipe is not the human oesophagus. To protect the user, this caution appears on the container:

"Danger. Harmful if swallowed, may burn eyes and mucous membranes on contact."

Marlboro manufacturers advertise their cigarettes with rustic, robust images. Advertisements portray a healthy, good looking muscular "he-man", sporting what many believe to be a cancer hazard from the corner of his mouth. The male model is so attractive, that it entices you to run to the nearest store for a packet of cigarettes, just so that you can look like the poster. To protect the consumer, a packet of *Marlboro* cigarettes carries this warning:

"Warning. The Surgeon General has determined that smoking is dangerous to your health."

Aerosol spray cans contain a number of products including air fresheners, hair spray, deodorant, perfume and paint. Most products carry a familiar caution:

"Physical Hazards. Contents under pressure. Do not use near fire, sparks or flame. Do not puncture or incinerate container ..."

Solid anti-perspirants like *Old Spice*, give users the following counsel:

"Caution. Do not apply to broken skin ... Keep this and all other drugs from the reach of children."

If human emotions and attitudes could be canned or packaged and sold across the grocer's counter, similar warning would be required. Legislation for controlling emotional reaction does exist. The bill was passed in the Divine Court of Law and is recorded in an official document called the Bible. The agency which enforces each law is the consequence of the violation. Human experience corroborates the accuracy of each law. Since it is the individual who chooses his emotions and actions in each given circumstance, it is wise to choose well. The following are some suggestions which might be required on the packages of personal reactions. For example:

The warning on a can of **Anger** might read:

"Use sparingly and in small amounts. Excessive use may cause symptoms ranging from high blood pressure to cerebral haemorrhage."

A package of **Bitterness** may warn:

"Long term use may cause reactions ranging from skin disorders to arthritis."

A six pack of **Hate** should read:

"Highly toxic. Can cause severe bodily injury or death."

A bag of **Worry** might warn:

"The Great Physician has determined that worry is the leading cause for numerous ailments ranging from migraine head-aches to stomach ulcers."

The warning label on a case of **Depression** would read:

"Highly contagious. May contaminate hope, purpose and productivity."

A litre of **Dissatisfaction** might assert:

"Habitual use will cause numerous personal, domestic and vocational irritations which may lead to major life style changes."

A package of **Assorted Emotions** may carry this disclaimer:

"The manufacturer disclaims any responsibility for any reactions the user may experience from this product."

The shelves in the emporium of emotional reactions are well stocked. Grouped in one section are the productive emotions, which include such choices as love, joy, peace, patience, kindness, generosity, fidelity, tolerance and self-control. They are stocked here because of the benefit they bring the user. Better than any health food, they produce a variety of advantages ranging from clear skin to low blood pressure.

Across the isle, grouped in the harmful emotions section, are lust, perverse thinking, intolerance, hatred, temper, contentiousness, jealousy, rivalry and envy. They are grouped together because of their toxic nature. They are known for producing eighty five percent of ailments which result in hospitalization. This includes a wide spectrum ranging from skin rashes to venereal disease. Many are terminal! The next time you visit the mercantile of human emotions, read the warning labels carefully before you choose. Please note the stock items found in the grocery list of Galatians 5:19-24:

> "*The acts of the sinful nature are obvious: sexual immorality, impurity and debauchery; idolatry and witchcraft; hatred, discord, jealousy, fits of rage, selfish ambition, dissensions, factions and envy; drunkenness, orgies, and the like. I warn you, as I did before, that those who live like this will not inherit the kingdom of God. But the fruit of the Spirit is love, joy, peace, patience, kindness, goodness, faithfulness, gentleness and self-control. Against such things there is no law. Those who belong to Christ Jesus have crucified the sinful nature with its passions and desires.*" *(New International Version)*

It becomes immediately noticeable that the shelves which carry harmful emotions are almost empty. Why should there be such a run on these items when they taste so bitter and their long-term effects are so harmful? Shopping carts are loaded and bags stuffed with poison. They may be colourfully wrapped and neatly packaged, but they are **poison**! The price paid for self-destruction is costly.

Near Detroit, Michigan, on the north side of highway 94, just a few miles from the Peace Bridge which leads to Canada, a huge billboard displays a three dimensional head of a beautiful cow. Her head is motorized to imitate the movements of a contented cow, peacefully chewing her cud. The caption beside her reads:

Contented cows give better milk!

Borden's mascot, "Elsie the Cow", has made millions for her company, and has impressed many thinking people with the reality of her cliches. Indeed, contented cows do give better milk. It is difficult to get milk from a cow that has just been chased by a pack of dogs. When this simple fact is extended to its practical application for daily living, the results are remarkable. It is also true that contented doctors make better surgeons. How would you like to have your appendix removed by a highly agitated, tense and driven surgeon? You might end up looking like a shish-kabob. It is also true that happy teachers make better instructors, gentle husbands make better fathers, tender wives make better mothers and satisfied workers make better employees. Joyful people make better friends. Honest people make better partners. Such people exert a positive influence on those around them and are therefore constantly surrounded by others. Note the admonition of Philippians 4:6-9:

"And now, my friends, all that is true, all that is noble, all that is just and pure, all that is lovable and gracious, whatever is excellent and admirable - fill all your thoughts with these things." - *(New English Bible)*

This is one key to successful living!

KEY 10   A HAPPY SPIRIT IS LIKE MEDICINE

She was helped into my office by two friends. She looked miserable! Her face winced under the disabling pain which was her constant companion. Her opening remarks underscored her misery:

"My body is crippling. My best day is when I hurt a lot. I am unable to stand or walk or sit or sleep ... I hate life!"

I ached with empathy for her, and wondered if there was anything I could do to help this poor creature of circumstance. Was there any hope or help for such a person? Is she indeed a creature of circumstance, or was there something she could do to take charge of her life? Surely, there must be some form of relief.

The dynamics which cause the illnesses people suffer are usually easy to identify. This is particularly true with physical sickness. The patient is preoccupied with the symptoms and seeks help from the professional. The professional diagnoses the cause and prescribes corrective measures. The same procedures are taken in dealing with emotional and psychological disorders. Present-day medical science and sophisticated technology are able to determine the source of the problem, but getting the person to do something about it is much more difficult. After patiently listening to her woes, I tried to explain one of the main characteristics of pain:

Physical pain is greatly aggravated by emotions and attitudes!

We cannot ignore the overwhelming statistics. It is conservatively estimated that fifty to eighty percent of all hospital beds are occupied by people suffering from psychosomatic disorders. Emotional and mental disorders are our nation's number one health problem. Eighty-five percent of all medication sold across our drug store counters are psychotropic (mind-altering, mood-controlling) in nature. The use of placebos (made of non-active materials) in medicine is widespread. Health care has become big business!

The startling fact is that the majority of these disorders can be avoided. Pain or discomfort is intensified by our emotions and attitudes. This colours our feelings to the point where we believe that we are suffering far more pain than we actually are. Here is a case in point. Suppose that your dental work is in need of repair. Your toothache is a physical problem caused by decay. This creates a persistent nagging pain. The pain is real, and your jaw hurts. But how do you measure pain? How would you respond to the question, "How much does it hurt?" Is it twelve inches (cm) of pain, four pounds (kg), three gallons (litre) or eighteen cubic feet of pain that you are enduring? There is no way to measure pain objectively. A pain measure simply does not exist. It quickly becomes evident that the only measurement for pain is your own subjective interpretation.

For the purpose of example, let us ascribe a co-efficient of "one unit" of pain to the toothache you are suffering. In addition to the "one unit" of physical pain, you also suffer from emotional and attitudinal reactions. It is difficult to be "chipper" or enthusiastic when your jaw throbs with each heartbeat. Your appetite is lost and your interest in a favourite pastime, in friends and in all projects wanes. How can you be objective when the gnawing pain diminishes every other interest into drab insignificance? Here is where the problem lies. In addition to the "one unit" of physical pain, you add corresponding emotional and attitudinal pain which may measure five, twenty, fifty or one hundred units. The total pain that is now felt is **one hundred and one units** of anguish, of which only one unit is physical.

1 Unit of Physical Pain, plus
20 Units of Emotional Pain, plus
50 Units of Attitudinal Pain, plus
30 Units of Relational Pain, equals

---

101 SUM TOTAL UNITS OF PAIN!

It hurts only as much as you let it!

I looked at the lady and said, "You are a very unhappy woman. Your unhappiness is a more serious problem than your physical condition." In due course she admitted to hating her husband, carrying bitterness towards her family, entertaining vengeful thoughts towards others and remembering every unkind word and act against her. "You cannot entertain these feelings and expect a healthy body!" I continued, "Your body is doing its best to counteract all the toxins you are flushing into your system, but it's losing the battle. If you don't change your attitude, your body will succumb!" The dynamics of her condition became clear to her and she asked, "What must I do?"

The question, *"What must I do?"* is the first step towards health and well-being. It acknowledges accountability and responsibility. To the man stricken with palsy, Jesus said:

> *"Son, be of good cheer; thy sins be forgiven thee ... Arise, take up thy bed, and go unto thine house." - Matthew 9:2+6*

Jesus addressed behavioural and emotional dynamics. With the recognition of the destructive causative factors (let's call them sins), comes acknowledgement. Once you recognize the problem and acknowledge it as being a cause, then corrective measures can be taken. For example, if the pin holes in your gluteus maxims are caused by the cactus on which you are sitting, the most prudent course of action is to **get off. Do something about it.** The action of doing something about it, is called by many names. It is known as **readjustment, removal, rectification or repentance**. Get rid of it! When the lady confessed her sins, she was forgiven. When she repented, she was freed from its corrupting effects. She asked her family and friends to forgive her. She changed her attitude towards herself and the world around her and became a happy person. Her new person became attractive to those around her and she developed new friends. Others came to her for counsel. And yes, her physical condition became so unimportant that she forgot about her problems and was indeed healed. Because the body was free from the stresses imposed upon it by harmful attitudes and destructive emotions, it functioned the way God had designed it to. It repaired itself! Such healing is truly Divine.

Listen to the instructions James gave the early Christian church. It would be wise for all of us to take note:

"Is any sick among you? Let him call for the elders of the church; and let them pray over him, anointing him with oil in the name of the Lord: And the prayer of faith shall save the sick, and the Lord shall raise him up; and if he has committed sins, they shall be forgiven him. Confess your faults one to another, and pray for one another, that ye may be healed." - James 5:14-16

This is one key to successful living!

KEY 11   POTENTIAL WRAPPED IN HUMAN SKIN

Most people never discover the fabulous potential which comes wrapped in human skin. The reference here, is to your skin.

In the city of Moose Jaw Saskatchewan, Canada, there lived a man who was affectionately called "Waldo, the weatherman". He was so identified because he lived in the out-doors in all types of weather, and was never seen without his full-length, sheepskin-lined overcoat. His home was his overcoat. He literally lived in it in the open air, whether it was the ninety degree heat of summer or the minus thirty degree cold of winter. It acted as an insulator protecting its resident. Feeling some responsibility for his welfare, the city paid for one hair cut each month and one meal a day at a local restaurant. As a lad growing up in the decade of the forties, I can still see him shuffling down the street with a pack of dogs following behind him.

It was not unusual for "Waldo, the weatherman" to miss a meal or two on occasion. But when five days went by without him coming in for his daily soup and meat loaf, the proprietor of the restaurant notified the authorities. The Royal Canadian Mounted Police were dispatched to the centre of the city's garbage dump where Waldo lived in two abandoned cars he had pulled together. One served as his bedroom and the other as his kitchen and living room. They found him stiff and horizontal. He had frozen to death in sub-zero temperatures.

Waldo's body was taken to the local morgue where he was thawed out in preparation for burial. When they removed his coat, they discovered the reason why he would never take it off. Pinned to the lining, they found ninety thousand dollars in cash! He had ninety thousand dollars in cash on his person, and he lived like a tramp. It is even more astounding when we remember that this occurred in the economy of fifty years ago. How utterly tragic.

He could have lived like a King. His money could have been multiplied into millions. He could have used his wealth to provide jobs and security for others. He could have used his influence to mould thought, life-styles, politics, philosophy and education. He could have been influential in city planning and government. He could have been a constant source of blessing to himself and those around him. But he lived like a vagrant and died like a tramp. No one really knew where he came from or who he was. He was a nameless nonentity who walked across the stage of life and vanished into oblivion. What a tragic overwhelming waste.

There are many lessons we can learn from his tragic example, but one stands out most clearly: wrapped in a bundle of flesh and pinned to the inside of human skin, is all the kinetic energy of the **divine potential!** Revelation 4:11 declares that "... _thou hast created all things, and for thy pleasure they are and were created._" As the object of His creative genius, you were made with purpose. Can Paul's declaration be any clearer?

> "_For we are his workmanship, created in Christ Jesus unto good works, which God hath before ordained that we should walk in them._"
> - _Ephesians 2:10_

Life is filled with fantastic potential. God's creative potential tabernacles within our beings! It was Norman Vincent Peale who said, "Put God to work for you and maximize your potential ..."

There are many, however, who will take that wealth and wrap it in a cloak of self-pity, feelings of inferiority, fear, apprehension, self-centredness, bitterness, hate and self-indulgence. They will choose to live among the junk of discarded failures, the rubbish of abandoned hopes, the trash of broken dreams and obsolete notions and the shards of fractured relationships. What overwhelming waste!

Paul, the Apostle, reminded the Ephesian Christians that they were chosen by God, accepted in the beloved and sealed with the Holy Spirit of promise. After he had established their desirable position, he made intercession for them, which is most interesting:

"I cease not to give thanks for you, making mention of you in my prayers; That the God of our Lord Jesus Christ, the Father of glory, may give unto you the spirit of wisdom and revelation in the knowledge of him: The eyes of your understanding being enlightened; that ye may know what is the hope of his calling, and what the riches of the glory of his inheritance in the saints, And what is the exceeding greatness of his power to us-ward who believe ..." - Ephesians 1:16-19

The majority of people never discover who they are or what they have been called to. Most people have no sense of purpose or destiny and live far below their potential. The Bible cites many examples of ordinary men and women who discovered who they were and achieved their destiny. Some of them were people of questionable reputation, but when they discovered the "hope of their calling" they became renowned.

A godless, uncircumcised, demon-worshipping Babylonian by the name of Abram discovered who he was, and became Abraham, the father of many nations. A cheating, lying scoundrel by the name of "Supplanter" stole his brother's birth right and his father-in-law's herd. When he discovered who he was, Jacob became Israel, a Prince with God. Rahab, a small town whore, discovered who she was, and became a vital link in the lineage of Jesus Christ. After the defeat of Jericho, Rahab married Salmon, one of Joshua's captains, and became the mother of Boaz, the Kinsman Redeemer who married Ruth. (Matthew 1:5) Rahab and Sarah are two women listed in the Hall of Fame in the book of Hebrews, chapter eleven. Jesus Christ has both a virgin and a harlot listed in his family tree.

It does not matter how big a failure you are or how big a sinner you may have become, it is encouraging to know that Jesus Christ is an even bigger Saviour! You may have failed miserably, but in Jesus Christ you can achieve your full potential. Your life pulsates with destiny. There is a life of beauty out there, worlds to discover, experiences to enjoy, new dreams to build, goals to achieve and relationships to establish. "I had ambition not only to go farther than any man had ever been before," said the discoverer, Captain James Cook, "but as far as it was possible for man to go!"

Come, let us move out to a new neighbourhood, the kingdom of God and His potential. Move away from the junk yard of past failures and disappointments. Leave the refuse dump of harmful memories, destructive emotions and bitter thinking. Peal off the coat which binds you and be set free!

Does this sound a bit like a sermon to you? I make no apology. It is good psychology, it is sound theology and it is great living for those who put these principles into practice!

This is one key to successful living!

KEY 12   HYPNOTIC POWERS WHICH BIND

"I feel like I am controlled by some hypnotic power. I'm like a pawn being moved inexorably toward defeat. What is worse, it is my own behaviour that is destroying me. I am my worst enemy!" These were the words of a 35 year old professional. He had gone through two marriages, two businesses and numerous churches. He had no friends or social life. His life was a dismal failure. "How can I get free from this thing that overpowers me?" he asked.

Your mind wields an enormous influence over your emotions and actions. This is illustrated by the strange phenomenon known as hypnosis. A brief study of its history is quite interesting.

In the mountain village of Kloster, Switzerland, lived a priest who had gifted powers for healing. When Father Gassner (1770) touched his parishioners with his metal cross, many were healed of physical, emotional and mental illnesses. Attending the "healing services" was a well-educated young man from an aristocratic family by the name of Franz Anton Mesmer. He had qualified himself in the disciplines of medicine, theology and law. A professional student by practice, he observed the process with intense curiosity. He reasoned that the unusual phenomenon had to have a logical explanation and determined to discover its secret. "If this dynamic works for a priest," he thought, "it should also work for a doctor. If it functions up in the mountains, it should operate in the valley, and if it performs well in a church yard, it should also do so in a clinical setting." He determined to duplicate the phenomenon in a clinical setting.

Mesmer theorized that every person was surrounded by fields of magnetic forces, much like a magnet. Man's illness, he concluded, was caused by a disruption of his "invisible magnetic fluids". He devised a plan to arrange these forces in their proper order. He hollowed out an oak log, and filled the tub-like cavity with bottles containing water. Iron chips and assorted pieces of metal which he found in a junk yard were also placed among the bottles. He contended that the bottles of water would absorb the "bad invisible magnetic fluids" and the metal fragments would give off "good invisible magnetic fluids".

No invisible magnetic fluids, but it worked!

His reasoning was erroneous and his method of treatment bizarre. The "magnetic fluids" were indeed invisible, simply because they did not exist! His techniques were unorthodox. This earned him much criticism and his eventual dismissal from the college of physicians. Despite his unfounded procedures, people from all over Europe came to recline on his bed of junk yard fragments. They were healed with astounding success! He became so widely known and his following so vast, that he was unable to treat all who came to him.

In sheer frustration, he left his office one day and proceeded to a nearby tree. In the presence of all his onlookers, he announced, "When I touch this tree with my cane, it will become *mesmerized*! All who touch it will be healed!" With that assertion, he returned to his office. It is a well-documented fact that as many as 3 000 people a day would visit Mesmer's tree. The majority of those who touched it were healed. This is not a story. It is documented fact. This strange phenomenon parades under several names, but it is most commonly known as "hypnosis".

Is there any logical explanation for this phenomenon? Yes indeed! Not all the aspects of mind-dynamics are clearly understood and it would be presumptuous to suggest a dogmatic answer. However, it is known that the mind exerts a powerful force and is the single most important factor in determining physical health, emotional stability, interpersonal relationships, personal aptitudes, skills and vocational efficiency. Solomon declared:

"As a man thinketh in his heart, so is he..." - Proverbs 23:7

The thought-process is a creative power controlled by each individual. This includes such dynamics as thought-patterns, ideas, concepts, mind-sets, attitudes, values and ideals. The converse is also true. Your thought-processes control you. In a very real way, you will become what you believe. The important question is, "How do you see yourself?" Whether you are accurate in your assessment or not, is irrelevant. If you envision yourself as a loser, then you are indeed a loser. This is not true because you are incapable of success, but because success is inconsistent with your thought-patterns. Failure is not only compatible with your thinking, but it is comforting in its misery. "After all," the loser concludes, "at least I am right in my assessment. I am a loser!" On the other hand, the person who sees himself as a winner will rise again, though he loses a dozen times. Loss must never be seen as defeat.

Success is incompatible with a loser's expectation !

He drove a new luxury car and was decked out with gold rings and chains. He already had three face-lifts and every tooth in his mouth was fitted with porcelain caps. His living-room displayed an eighteen thousand dollar Steinway piano, and a special galley was built unto his house to accommodate his pipe organ. Despite all his affluence, Sam was a forty year old failure. He came to my office for relief and direction. "I feel like such a failure! I feel so totally worthless! I feel like such a loser!" After listening to his litany of woes, I tried to encourage him. "Look Sam," I said, "you have to be more positive than that." Looking blank and nondescript he replied, "All right. I **know** that I am a failure!" That was not the point I was trying to make. What do you tell a man who has totally hypnotized himself into failure? The dynamics of this mind-controlling phenomenon are simple:

1. CONSCIOUSNESS IS NARROWED

If you focus intently upon any object, event or concept, everything else will diminish into insignificance. Every other concern fades into the background. This is true in every area of life, whether it be a good book, a TV special, a football game, an idea, a project, a relationship or an event. Nothing else appears important. Everything other than the preoccupation becomes irrelevant.

2. ALTERED ATTENTIVENESS IS PRODUCED

So all-consuming and pre-occupied is your thinking, that all other interests appear non-existent. All attentiveness is directed toward the central focal point of your pre-occupation. All other options and contingencies are ignored. In effect, a state of altered consciousness is produced where your attention is focussed on less and less, until you see everything about nothing!

3. SUSCEPTIBILITY TO SUGGESTION OCCURS

Because all other concerns have little relevance, you become blinded to the real facts and can only accept information which may corroborate the pre-occupation.

4. A CONCEPT IS PRESENTED

An addiction develops as desire for more of the fixation increases. Because you are so desirous for more, your mind becomes wide open towards anything which may feed the obsession. The mind will then accept a new concept without testing the reality or verifying genuineness. In this way, many people are convinced against their better judgment, resulting in incongruous thinking and dysfunctional behaviour.

5. BEHAVIOUR IS CONTROLLED

Reality then assumes the format that the concept establishes. Reality is no longer a world of objects or things as they exist, but a world as you perceive it to be. It has been said that "beauty is in the eye of the beholder." The fact is that your mind tells you what is real about life. The Bible clearly warns us about the hypnotic powers which seek to control us, and what we can do about it:

> *"But I fear, lest by any means, as the serpent beguiled (deceived, fooled, hypnotized) Eve through his subtlety, so your **minds** should be corrupted from the simplicity that is in Christ." - 2 Corinthians 11:3*

Eve's progression to deception can be listed in light alliteration. Eve **Loitered** in the presence of temptation, she **Lingered Longer** than was wise, she **Listened** to the Tempter, **Looked** at his offer, **Lessened** her guard, **Liked** what she saw, **Lusted** after the forbidden and **Latched** unto the deception. Satan is called the Deceiver. He takes the skin of a truth and stuffs it with insinuations, innuendos, misconceptions and blatant lies! He is a master at misrepresenting the truth. Aristotle made reference to the authors in his time with these uncomplimentary words, "Homer has taught all other poets the art of telling lies skilfully." When a concept is presented that is contrary to the teaching of God's Word, get out! In this way you will avoid deception. Paul gives a valuable antidote to those who have been afflicted with deception:

> *"For the weapons of our warfare are not carnal, but mighty through God to the **pulling down of strongholds; casting down imaginations, and every high thing that exalteth itself against the knowledge of God, and bringing into captivity every thought to the obedience of Christ."**- 2 Corinthians 10:4-5*

All healing comes from God. He tells us that much of our healing can be brought about by proper thinking. "Unhypnotize" yourself! Let your thought-process be controlled by Jesus Christ and His teachings, rather than by your fears, harmful attitudes, negative feelings, adverse circumstances or imaginations. Despite life's difficulties, learn to see its beauties. Life is beautiful! You are free to enjoy life in its fullest dimension. Believe it.

This is one key to successful living!

KEY 13 WHAT HAPPENED TO SOUND THINKING?

What ever happened to sound thinking? There was a time when thinking was synonymous with well-doing. If a certain value or process could be proven as true, it was accepted as fact and acted upon. The internal combustion engine, for example, was designed to operate on gasoline. It would be senseless to fill the fuel tank with ordinary water. All you have to do to keep from hitching a ride to the nearest fuel station, is to comply with this obvious fact. It is also a fact that by shoving a carrot in your ear, your hearing will be impaired and serious damage may be caused to the inner ear. It also looks stupid. Therefore it is logical that a prudent course of action would be not to be seen with a garden carrot projecting from your ear. It would be considered sound thinking to follow this principle.

Modern day society, however, has advanced far beyond this infantile form of reasoning. The aberrations of human logic need not call for action. Instead, it fosters debate about philosophy, politics, sociology, values, ethics and man's inalienable rights. It might well be proven for example, that sporting an organic carrot from your ear impairs hearing, may seriously damage the ear drum, and looks stupid, but it is your right to wear what you want, when you want, where you want! "This is my body! I am a consenting adult! I am a free moral agent! No one has the right to impose his moral standards on anyone else, and I will freely do what I so please!" asserted one liberated free-thinker. The natural outcome is to proudly display the carrot of independence, protruding from the ear. For some strange reason, this type of logic is applauded as being "astute, spot on, in the now!" In reality, it is one short step from insanity. Napoleon alluded to this when he said, "In politics stupidity is not a handicap!"

Having exercised his human rights, the emancipated one becomes concerned about his loss of hearing, constant dizziness, fever and head colds. He is also troubled about his sudden drop in popularity. In a sincere attempt to determine the cause, he books appointments with his medical practitioner and psychiatrist. Those who follow this course of action are **really with it** ! They contend that this is "contemporary pragmatic thinking, the philosophy of the future." This type of logic is illustrated by the patient who went to see his psychologist brandishing a carrot in his ear. The doctor, looking quizzically at his patient, asked, "Do you know that you have a carrot hanging from your ear?" "Oh yes!" replied the patient. "But why do you do that?" asked the doctor. "Well, you see, I was fresh out of celery!" It has been said that a sinner can reform, but stupidity is forever! Totally illogical and incongruous, it makes no difference to this patient. It is his right to do what he wants.

What has happened to sound reasoning that produces sound behaviour? Jesus declared, "*If you know these things, happy are you if you do them!*" - John 13:17. James asserted, "*Be ye* **doers** *of the word, and not hearers only!*" - James 1:22. Why is it so difficult for "modern man" to submit himself to a set of proven principles? Is obedience a sign of weakness? Is the act of submission synonymous with emasculation? Is exaggerated independence to be seen as strength and maturity? Is reckless indifference to be admired as macho? Is defiant rebellion to be admired? **No!** With the sound of a thousand voices, **No!** Any horse can kick, any dog can bark and any bull can charge. Any animal can rip and tear. But it takes a person of mature character and greatness to evaluate reality in the light of evidence and to submit to its outcome. Solomon put it rather strongly:

"The way of a fool is right in his own eyes; but he that hearkeneth unto counsel is wise." - Proverbs 12:15

The majority of people have carrots protruding from the strangest places. The carrot may be emotional in nature. It may be behavioral, traditional, attitudinal, dispositional, relational, vocational or some other personal dynamic. As accustomed as you have become to wearing it, **get rid of it** ! It is ungainly, infectious and most inconvenient. It also looks absurd.

There are those who sincerely ask, "What do I do to get rid of this problem?" The answer is simple: "Submit yourself to a proven standard!" "But where do I find such a standard?" you ask. There are two standards. The first is valuable, the second is absolute. One is subjective, the other is objective.

1. THE SUBJECTIVE STANDARD

The subjective standard is your own conscience. Everyone has within himself, a sense of what is right and what is wrong. There are no amoral people, but many people live in violation of their own standard of what is right. When this is done, insensitivity to your own conscience builds up, until its voice is no longer heard. Do what you know is right. Paul, the apostle, charged the whole world as guilty before God, because they had violated the testimony of their own conscience:

"For the wrath of God is revealed from heaven against all ungodliness and unrighteousness of men, who hold the truth in unrighteousness; Because that which may be known of God is manifest in them (known within man's conscience); for God hath shewed it unto them." - Romans 1:18-19

2. THE OBJECTIVE STANDARD

The objective standard is God's revelation to man. He who created man and woman, has also provided them with an operator's manual. It is the guide's map for life and it guarantees optimum living. It is called the

Bible. God's Word is as authentic as His character, therefore it is an indispensable tool for life. Follow its directions carefully.

> *"This book of the law shall not depart out of thy mouth; but thou shalt meditate therein day and night, that thou mayest observe to do according to all that is written therein: for then thou shalt make thy way prosperous, and then thou shalt have good success." - Joshua 1:8*

This is one key to successful living!

KEY 14   SLAVE TO THE ORDINARY

"Every day is SOT! I awaken in the morning expecting and knowing that it will be SOT. It has always been this way. It will never change! It's always sot, Sot, SOT!" This was the sentiment which was expressed by a house wife who came for counsel. SOT is an acronym for the **Same Old Thing!** As a professional counsellor of more than thirty-five years, SOT has come to my office in different bodies, dressed in different attire, from different life styles, wearing different faces and complaining about the **Same Old Thing!**

There are many people in this world who are slaves to the ordinary. SOT is a prison house of mundane routine, shattered hopes, frustrating circumstances, unexpected reversals and fruitless efforts. The ordinary has become a ball and chain of boring expectations. Solomon put it succinctly when he said, "... *There is no new thing under the sun.*" - Ecclesiastes 1:9. He was right! "Under the sun", it's just plain every day SOT. But there is a dimension which is beyond the sun, beyond sensory perception and far above the disappointments of daily circumstances.

Under the sun or in the Son?

The story of Noah provides a great deal of encouragement. The narrative is found in Genesis 7-9. He single-handedly built the ark, while warning his peers of impending judgment. Not one supporting hand was offered him. For 120 years he faithfully laboured alone. Not one convert was gained. Only his offspring believed his message. The only reward he received was aching muscles and criticism, malicious, denigrating opposition which still can be heard:

> "The old man has to be crazy! Building that monstrosity in our fashionable neighbourhood is insane. It's three hundred miles (km) from the nearest body of water. What's he going to do when he finishes it? Pull it over there? It will be easier to dig a trench and bring the water here!"

Finally the craft was completed, standing higher than a four story building and overlapping a football field on all sides. The animals entered and Noah set journey on his shoreless ocean. If Noah was alive today, he would surely be chosen by the President to serve as advisor on economic affairs. You must remember, Noah floated his stock, while the rest of the world was liquidated!

As a child, I would read this story and envision the romantic adventure. Noah and his wife, their three sons and their wives, playing *Scrabble, Uno* or *Monopoly* in the evening by lamp light. A calf chewing its cud nearby, a cat purring on someone's lap and ducks nesting for the night in a mound of hay. The chickens roosting in the rafters above; how romantic, peacefully cosy. As an adult, I came to discover that what Noah was navigating was a floating barn-yard including the manure pile! I was reared on the farm. My understanding of this event is quite realistic. As a lad, I was required to milk seven cows before I went to school. I was given no **udder** choice! I am well aware of the bedding and cleaning seven cows require. Noah's chores included caring for camels, elephants, rhinos and the like. The story ends with these words:

> *"And the* **ark** *rested ... upon the mountains of Ararat ... and* **the tops of the mountains were seen !** *" - Genesis 8:4-5.*

Make a conscious note of this certainty, **it is impossible to see the tops of the mountains when you are looking down at the manure** ! I can envision this hypothetical Noahic SOT scenario:

"Listen Lord, I've been obedient to you! It took me 120 years to build this, this, this ... "**Aquazoo**" for you. Now for more than a year you've penned me up with these turkeys ... and pigs and skunks. I'm tired of this SOT, cleaning, bedding, exercising, feeding, watering, brushing, shóvelling. I've had it up to **here** with these cramped quarters. It's hot and humid. I'm in a state of perpetual sea sickness with this constant yawing and pitching. All this makes me nauseous! And besides this, it smells. Look at all this stuff!"

Can you identify with this feeling? Surely! We know exactly how he must have felt. But the story has a different ending. He patiently carried out God's directives for more than 120 years, with no support or encouragement. All he had was **hope** and **faith** in a vision. He knew there were better things to come. And because his vision was focused upon the mountain tops and the promises of God, the SOT of daily living made no difference. Incidently, there is no evidence to support the theory that it was Noah who coined the phrase "Poop-deck"!

Be of good cheer "Ye slaves of SOT." Emancipation is here. No longer will this taskmaster loom over you with the propensities of an evil monster. There is a passage-way to escape. Follow these simple steps:

1. REFOCUS YOUR VISION

Get your eyes off your circumstances. Every trial has an ending. Every difficult circumstance has a built-in self-destruct mechanism. It can't last forever! "*I will lift mine eyes unto the hills,*" declared King David in Psalm 121:1-2. Then he added, "*From whence cometh my help? My help cometh from the Lord.*" Focus your vision on the exciting future with its potential and the possibilities that lie within you.   "Democracy," said H E Fosdick, "is based upon the conviction that there are extraordinary possibilities in ordinary people."

2. CUT YOUR PROBLEMS DOWN TO SIZE

As horrendous as your circumstances may appear, they are smaller than your ability to handle them. Never be intimidated by your problems. Don't be afraid to tackle your predicament. "Life without courage for death is slavery," said Seneca. You have endured it thus far. You are strong enough to handle it.

3. LIFT YOUR FACE UNTO THE MOUNTAIN-TOPS

Follow the examples set by our forefathers. They endured loneliness, uncertainty and unspeakable hardships, but it led to new discoveries, without which we would be severely disadvantaged. Paul, the Apostle, and James, the brother of Jesus, admonished the early Christian church with these words:

> *"Looking unto Jesus the author and finisher of our faith ... For consider him ... lest ye be wearied and faint in your minds." - Hebrews 12:2-3.*

> *"My brethren, count it all joy when ye fall into divers temptations; Knowing this, that the trying of your faith worketh patience. But let patience have her perfect work, that ye may be perfect and entire, wanting nothing!" - James 1:2-4*

4. ANTICIPATE THE BEST FROM LIFE

In a sense expectation is self-fulfilling. You usually find what you are looking for. You will see the very thing you are searching for. Forget the barn-yard cleanings and elevate your vision. Look for the unusual, the exciting, the unexpected. Try something new and expect the best from life. There is a reality beyond the tedium of SOT, and it is available for all who want it. "Depend on it," said Sir Arthur C Doyle, "there is nothing so unnatural as the commonplace."

This is one key to successful living!

KEY 15   AN ANTIDOTE FOR ILLNESS

Forgiveness is an outstanding antidote for illness. It benefits the one forgiven, but it benefits the one who forgives even more. *The Toronto Daily Star* carried a human interest story of an eighty-six year old man who lived a miserable life and died a painful death. What made this man's death newsworthy, were his little black books. Boxes stacked ceiling high and filled with little black books. He always carried a little black book in his shirt pocket, in which he recorded every unkind word, inconsiderate act and painful incident his wife "inflicted on him". When death finally came, it came as a sweet messenger of peace bringing relief to everyone, especially to himself! They found among his meagre possessions a veritable library of black, hand-written books, containing fifty-six years of bitterness, vengefulness and hate. He lived a lonely, painful life and died a solitary death. No one came to his funeral, not even his family.

Would it not have been better if he had carried a white book, in which he recorded all the good deeds his wife and friends may have shown him? The advantages are immediately evident. First, he would have had fewer entries to make. Second, he would have had fewer books to cart around and store. Third, the weight of bitterness, self-pity, hate and vengefulness would not have been so burdensome. Fourth, he would have lived a happy life. He also may have had someone willing to read his eulogy.

In Matthew 18:21-22 Peter asked our Lord, *"How oft shall my brother sin against me, and I forgive him?"* Jesus replied, *"seventy times seven."*

That's 490 times! Four hundred and ninety times? What kind of person would endure abuse without objection? A person would have to be a masochist to allow injustice to go on unchallenged. Four hundred and ninety times?

Let us be genuine as well as practical. What would you do if someone stepped on your toes inadvertently and begged for your forgiveness? Would you forgive him? Certainly! Suppose that five minutes later he stepped on your toes again, then profusely apologized? You would probably forgive him again. But what would you do if ten minutes later he tripped over your feet a third time and again expressed his remorse? By now you would be sitting on the chair with your feet tucked under you. Your patience would likely endure and once again you would forgive him. But what if yet another time he bumped into your chair, knocked you to the floor, and stomped his entire weight on your feet. Would you now forgive him? Would you benignly excuse his behaviour as a lack of coordination, or would you let him have it with all the "gusto of a nickel-plate freight?" Probably the latter!

Forgive - 490 times?

We are instructed to forgive such a person. Why? In the name of sound reasoning, why should anyone forgive such a clumsy oaf? He is not worthy of forgiveness. No, he isn't. His well-earned dues may be some form of retaliation. Such a bungling person is worthy of a straight-jacket and padded cell to ensure his protection and the welfare of everyone else around him. Nevertheless, Jesus instructs us to forgive him, and for some very good reasons. There are several interesting facts about forgiveness.

1. FORGIVENESS IS NOT EARNED

The dynamics of forgiveness is not contingent upon worthiness. No one can earn forgiveness, it can only be received. Be thankful that God does not treat us according to our earned rewards, but rather according to His mercy. If God forgave us in direct proportion to our earnings, none would be saved. In the Lord's prayer, Jesus taught the disciples to pray,

"Forgive us our debts (trespasses), as (in the same measure) we forgive our debtors (those who have trespassed against us.)" - Matthew 6:12. Philip James Bailey stated that *"They who forgive most, shall be most forgiven!"*

2. FORGIVENESS BENEFITS THE ONE WHO FORGIVES

Forgiveness benefits the forgiver much more than the "forgivee". The antonym of forgiveness is bitterness, anger, hate, hostility and vengefulness. Those who do not forgive, carry with them these extremely destructive emotions. They who harbour such toxic emotions will be destroyed by them. The lack of forgiveness is corrosive. It will slowly eat at you until it consumes you entirely. The one who does not forgive is the loser. He is like the youngster who flipped a coin in the air and called, "Heads, I win! Tails, you lose!" In either case, his friend is a loser. If you forgive, you may lose face and suffer some inconvenience. If you do not forgive, you lose infinitely more! This is the import of Hebrews 12:15:

"... lest any man fail of the grace of God; lest any root of bitterness springing up trouble you, and thereby many be defiled."

Rev James Reid heads a hospital ministry in Houston Texas. At a recent convention for therapists and counsellors, Mr Reid asked, "What, in your opinion, ladies and gentlemen, is the leading cause for physical and mental disorders?" He was surprised to learn that ninety-two percent responded with a single characteristic: a lack of forgiveness, an unwillingness or inability to forgive!

3. FORGIVENESS AIDS THE HEALING PROCESS

The human brain is responsible for manufacturing some eighty-six different secretions, necessary for healthy and efficient functioning of the body. Examples are numerous. The salivary glands respond to the smell of a well-cooked meal; adrenalin is pumped into the system in emergency situations; and tears moisten the eyes for various reasons. At the base of the brain is a small gland which produces a lubricant necessary for the joints of the body. It has been discovered that the switch which starts the process is an emotional device called "happiness". Medical science is well aware of the fact that bitterness, hate, unhappiness and vengefulness are leading contributing factors for numerous physical disorders ranging from arthritis to colitis.

Endorphin, which is found only in the human body, is a more powerful pain killer than morphine and a better antibiotic than penicillin. Endorphin is found in abundance in the bodies of happy people. Traces of endorphin are negligible in the bodies of bitter, unhappy, hateful and vengeful people. The lesson is clear. Learn to laugh and be happy. Grow your own endorphin and be healthy. "One must laugh before one is happy," said Jean De La Brugere, "or one may die without ever laughing!"

Culture your own endorphin and be healthy!

Be grateful to God for your sense of humour and the gift of laughter. If you lack a joyful disposition, ask the Lord to give you one. May the Lord smite us with happiness, and may we never recover.

It is not without cause or sound reason that Jesus said, "Forgive your enemies 490 times." There are defensive measures that can be taken when confronted by an assailant, but they do not include bitterness, self-pity or vengefulness. Solomon could well have received a doctorate for his research which concluded that:

> *"A merry heart doeth good like a medicine: but a broken spirit drieth the bones." - Proverbs 17:22*

"A merry heart maketh a cheerful countenance: but by sorrow of the heart the spirit is broken." - Proverbs 15:13

This is one key to successful living!

KEY 16   IMAGINATION: A CREATIVE FORCE

The **imagination** is the most powerful force known to mankind. Imagination is the ability to form a mental image of something not present or never before seen in reality. Evidence of its marvels are seen everywhere, including such achievements as man's ability to travel at five times the speed of sound, walk on other planets, see through solid materials, hear across continents, live in multi-storied high-rises and cook without heat. All this existed only as an imaginary concept in some fertile mind. It was later detailed in blue prints and then engineered into material shapes. Whether it be a process, event, relationship or material object, everything began initially as an imaginary thought. The creativity and power of the imagination is without limitation. It has been said that, **whatever you can conceive, you can achieve !**

Imagination can be used for its destructive potential as well as its beneficial resources. The example of a sharp kitchen knife illustrates this point. A knife can be used for cutting, whittling, carving, shaping, loosing and slicing. The task of slicing a tomato requires a sharp knife. You do not slice a tomato with a butter knife. A tomato can only be squashed with a butter knife. The sharper the knife, the better it is for cutting tomatoes. It is also true, however, that the sharper the knife, the more dangerous it is for cutting fingers. The same sharp edge cuts fingers and hands as well as tomatoes. A knife's potential for good or harm is equally great. So it is with the imagination. It is sadly true that many people use this force more frequently for their hurt than for their good.

We often use our imagination harmfully against ourselves. We entertain thoughts which create fear, worry, ineffectiveness, sickness, stress and failure. Whether used purposely, ignorantly or unwittingly, the force of imagination moves us inexorably towards success or failure. It is time that we understood the resources available to us, and use them for creative purposes.

Everyone has experienced the power of imagination. Have you ever tried to go to sleep, but every effort fails? Your best resolve ends in wide-eyed insomnia. Has an urge to laugh ever overtaken you in a solemn place? Your best determination to stop ends with audible nasal snorts. The harder you try to regain composure, the more you giggle. Have you ever tried to stop a nagging cough, or remember a familiar name, or free yourself from a persistent thought, or recall something you have forgotten? Indeed! This experience is known by everyone. Your best resolve declares, "I won't!" Your imagination asserts, "Yes you will! See, you are!" The reason for this truth is that the imagination is more powerful than the will.

Whenever the will is pitted against the imagination, it is always the imagination that will win. This principle is absolute. It permits no exception. The concept that man is a morally free agent, capable of voluntary choice, must be re-thought. Man's **will** is dominated by his **imagination**. To this the scriptures attest:

"For as a man thinketh in his heart, so is he." - *Proverbs 23:7*

Ask the alcoholic if he has ever tried to stop drinking. Every drink an alcoholic takes, is his last. He will tell you that he has tried time and time again; that he hates his life-style and desires a change. He will also confess that even if his next drink would catapult him immediately into Hell, he would still be impelled by some strange force to take just one more drink. Ask the overweight person if he has ever been on a diet, the smoker if he has ever tried to quit, the worrier if he has ever tried to stop worrying? Without exception, they will tell you that their best resolve is of little value.

The imagination is more powerful than the will.

This would indeed be depressing, were it not for the encouraging words of 2 Corinthians 10:4-5. Here we find the key to self-control:

"For the weapons of our warfare (are you fighting against some problem?) are not carnal (of human will or effort), but mighty through God (the Provider of every means) to the pulling down of strong holds (that problem which has resisted your best resolve); Casting down **imaginations** *(those mental images which control you), and every high thing that exalteth itself against the knowledge of God (every dynamic which controls you, contrary to God's purpose in your life) and bringing into captivity every thought to the obedience of Christ."*

Thought-functions include such processes as imagination, mind-sets, memories, ideas, ideals, concepts, data, values and bits and pieces of happenings. These must all be brought under control of and in line with God's Word. Herein lies one of the keys to successful living. If you imagine yourself to be a failure, it is a certainty that you will never succeed. If, however, you see yourself as God sees you, your potential is unlimited.

Some pointed questions must be asked: "Is your imagination working in your life? Is your will working in cooperation with your imagination for creative purposes? Is your imagination striving at cross-purposes with your will, resulting in failure?" Here are several suggestions that will help you use your imagination for productive purposes.

1. FAILURE IS INCONSISTENT WITH SUCCESS

The concept of failure is inconsistent with success. You must recognize that the notion of failure is contrary to **fact**. Failure must be seen as mid-course corrections on the way to success. The thought of failure is also an affront to the teachings of scripture. The Bible declares that, *"we are more than conquerors through Him,"* that we *"... are His workmanship created in Christ Jesus unto good works,"* that *"If these things be in you, and abound, they make you that ye shall neither be barren nor unfruitful in the knowledge of Christ!"* You must command your mind to imagine these declarations. It is an offence to think that God, who created us as his ultimate achievement, is pleased with the concept of failure, deficiency and ineffectiveness.

2. FAILURE MUST BE REJECTED

Life offers many unpleasant experiences. Some can be very ugly and damaging, leaving behind emotional and mental scars which are evident long after the body has healed and the circumstances have been resolved. The lingering pre-occupation with painful memories produces a conditioning effect which results in dysfunctional attitudes, behaviour and relationships. Furthermore, the memory of the event has become so distorted, and has grown to such proportions, that it no longer represents the actual incident. Such painful memories must be repulsed. You must choose to remember it differently. You must tear down every false imagination. Fabled imaginations are destructive. Stop envisioning or thinking about the fearful and the painful. The testimony of the Apostle Paul, in Philippians 3:13-14, gives us the key to successful living:

"... But one thing I do: Forgetting what is behind and straining toward what is ahead, I press on toward the goal to win the prize for which God has called me ..." (New International Version)

3. REPLACE FAILURE WITH HIGH IDEALS

You must replace harmful thoughts with proper thinking, with imaginations which are truly founded in God. In this way, self-confidence becomes energized by God-confidence. You will discover that your doubts and insecurities will give way to assurance and boldness. It is imperative that every person has this assurance. Without it, success is an impossibility. Be careful that you do not confuse this approach with positive thinking. Positive thinking is superior to negative thinking. The weakness of positive thinking, however, is that it may easily be corrupted by denial. This is **factual thinking** because it is based on the Word of God, and is therefore far more superior. When you envision the **factual imagery** of who you are in Christ Jesus, you will be able to accomplish the *"good works"* God has planned for your life.

4. DETERMINE A COURSE OF ACTION

Once the area of need is established, a **specific plan of action** must be determined. Be detailed in **what** you are going to do about it; **how** you are going to bring this about; **where** this process is going to take place; **how much it will cost** in terms of time, money and effort; **who** will be affected; **what resources** you have and **where** you can get help. In simple terms:

Plan your work, then work your plan!

5. DECLARE YOUR GOALS OPENLY

Upon your thoughtful and prayerful examination, **declare your intention.** Much like unspoken prayer requests which have unspoken answers, secret convictions seldom carry through to fruition. Since no one knows about them, no one will know when you give up trying. Private resolves encourage failure. A public declaration of your conviction is a catalyst for success. Your choice to purchase a new car, for example, will be publicly seen. You cannot keep something like that secret unless you plan to store the car under wraps. Once your signature is on the bank loan, you have nothing left to do but to pay the monthly instalments faithfully. You now have the responsibility of honouring your loan commitment and maintaining your new acquisition, but you also have the privilege of driving a new car.

6. START NOW

Getting started is eighty-five percent of the project. Why not start now? Is there any reason why **now** is not a good time to begin? Tomorrow is a poor time to begin, simply because there is no tomorrow. No one has ever seen tomorrow. Most people are slaves to an erroneous concept of time. The result is that the project never gets started. We are taught that time is divided into past, present and future. The past is only a memory, a 35 mm slide, a tape recording. The past does not exist. The future does not exist. It has not happened. All you have is **now**! In view of this fact, the prudent course of action is to get motivated. Do it now. It is for this reason that we are challenged with these words:

"Now is that accepted time! Today is the day of salvation."
- 2 Corinthians 6:2

7. DON'T BE HESITANT TO ASK FOR HELP

No person is an island unto himself. Because we are social beings, we need the encouragement of others. Therefore it is important to solicit help. Find a support group or a friend you can trust. Better still, find a church that is alive and become part of its growth. It is important to laugh with those who laugh, and cry with those who cry. They will encourage you when you find yourself faint and weary. They will also find strength from your courage. Relatives, close friends, prayer groups or Bible study groups, and others who have the same need, make excellent support groups.

8. DO NOT WEARY UNDER OPPOSITION

Expect reversals! The only way to learn how to skate or ski is to get up every time you fall. Solomon stated that a good man will fall many times, and get up again. One thing is certain, your falls will aid you in developing your landing skills. They also shorten the recycling time (getting back on your feet), lengthen the playing period and establish confidence in your routine. Never become discouraged because of reversals and setbacks. A faulty attempt must never be viewed as failure.

Learn to emphasise the word **attempt,** rather than the word **faulty.** "Even a mistake," said Henry Ford, "may turn out to be the one thing necessary for a worthwhile achievement."

9. BE PROUD OF YOUR ACHIEVEMENTS

Be happy with your successes, even if they fall short of your expectations. This was expressed well by one who planned to lose 50 pounds (22 kg) but had succeeded in losing only 30 (13 kg), "I may not be what I desire to be, but I thank God that I'm not what I used to be! By His strength I will become what He desires me to be!" Such determination is exhilarating. "I know the price of success," said Frank Lloyd Wright: "dedication, hard work and an unremitting devotion to the things you want to happen."

10. DISCOVER AN EVER EMERGING NEW YOU

A trust in God and an obedience to his Word will result in victory. Self-examination, honesty and determination are the means. Grover Cleveland summarized this well when he said; "Unswerving loyalty to duty, constant devotion to truth, and a clear conscience will overcome every discouragement and surely lead the way to usefulness and high achievement."

This is one key to successful living!

KEY 17   PHYSICIAN, HEAL THYSELF

Jesus asked the paralytic, "Do you want to be healed?" What a question to ask! The answer is obvious, don't you think? Does anyone enjoy a crippling handicap? What advantage is there to any disability? What pleasure can anyone derive from sickness? The answer would be obvious, except for the fact that Jesus never asked an empty question.

The truth is that there are many benefits which can be derived from disability. Sickness places its victim at the centre of attention where sympathy can be expunged from all who may pass by. While others queue in line and wait for their turn, the sick are carried in preferential ease to the front of the line. Others earn a living by the sweat of their brow, while the sick are tenderly cared for. The healthy person is preoccupied with the tedium of mundane chores and concerns of daily living. The sick have no responsibility to concern them.

This is not intended to be a disparaging reflection on the sick or handicapped. No healthy person would exchange his place with the infirm. Furthermore, it is our duty and privilege to support the less fortunate. It is one of God's commands:

"Is not this the fast that I have chosen? to loose the bands of wickedness, to undo the heavy burdens, and to let the oppressed go

free, and that ye break every yoke? Is it not to deal thy bread to the hungry, and that thou bring the poor that are cast out to thy house? when thou seest the naked, that thou cover him; and that thou hide not thyself from thine own flesh? (Note the results.) Then shall thy light break forth as the morning, and thine health shall spring forth speedily: and thy righteousness shall go before thee; the glory of the Lord shall be thy reward. Then shalt thou call, and the Lord shall answer; thou shalt cry, and he shall say, Here I am ..." - Isaiah 58:6-9

There are many people, however, who use their illness for ulterior purposes. Sickness can be used to cover a variety of unhealthy attitudes and traits ranging from irresponsibility to slothfulness, from fearfulness to obsequious self-centredness, and from reckless indifference to outright rebellion. Sickness can become a grand excuse. When Jesus asked the thought-provoking question, "Sir, do you want to be healed?" He stripped off the veneer of comforting illusion and sheltered half truths, which will forever keep you sick.

The question posed to you is: "Sir, Madam, do you want to be healed?" If so, then "Physician, heal thyself!" The following statistics write a glaring commentary on our present day social structure:

*   Two out of every five marriages end in divorce.

*   Of the two remaining, only one has any semblance of happiness.

*   A teacher in a school of 2 200 students stated, "72% of the entire student body comes from broken homes, single parent homes, or homes where a stepparent is involved!"

*   A city of 2 million people reports that 55% of its working force are single adults.

*   More people are incapacitated by emotional and mental disorders than by all other health problems combined.

* 85% of all prescriptions written by the medical profession are psychotropic - mind- and mood-altering.

* Tranquilizers sold across our drug store counters measure in the hundreds of tons (kilograms).

* One state in America reported more abortions than births.

* For the first time in history, more dissolutions of marriages were recorded by our courts than marriages.

* Mental and emotional disorders have become our nation's "number one health problem".

* *US and World News* carried an article which described marriage in today's society as "conjugal succession".

Each one of these statistics is documented. Behavioral scientists have termed our present day society as a "social nightmare". What is most alarming, however, is that 95% of the problems are self-imposed. It is like finding a man lying by the road-side, bruised and bleeding from a violent beating. After nursing him back to health and strength you discover that the thrashing he received was self-inflicted with a club he had found in the ditch. Sick? Yes indeed! Perhaps this is the reason why behavioral scientists see ours as a "sick society!"

Yet, there is a seed of hope in this sad melee. Since it is true that the majority of the problems are self-imposed, it is also true that the majority of the problems are self-corrected. Jesus quotes an ancient proverb while addressing a group of religious leaders, *"Physician, heal thyself."* - Luke 4:23. The fact is that **most healing is self-inspired!** A couple can have a healthy home, if they genuinely want it. They can have a beautiful marriage, if they sincerely long for it. A person can have a healthy attitude or mind-set, if he truly desires it. A person can go to bed and sleep with the serenity of a child, if he earnestly wants it. There is no problem in life so overwhelming that a workable solution cannot

be found. Here is encouraging news. Healing is available to all who
want it. It is a matter of obedience and submission to simple rules.

Most healing is self-influenced.

The measure of your desire, or your **want to,** is determined by your
actions. The Apostle Paul underscores this fact succinctly with this
instruction:

> "*Those things, which ye have both learned, and received, and heard,
> and seen in me,* **do : and the God of peace shall be with you.**" -
> *Philippians 4:9*

There are many elements which hinder healing, but pride is the most
important factor. You cannot afford pride. It is far too expensive a
commodity to own. It is arrogant pride which prevents a man from
saying, "I'm sorry honey, I really blew it," or "I confess that the
responsibility is mine," or "I guess I have to change in this area." Even
the words, "I'm sorry. Please forgive me," or "I am wrong," tend to stick
in our throats. It is loathsome pride which stops a person from seeking
needed help, or obeying a law, or submitting to an authority. It is
offensive pride which restrains a person from falling on his knees before
God in prayer, "Lord, help! I need your direction." It is repugnant pride
which resists the process needed for well-being.

Pride comes masked in many forms: personal dominance, pseudo-
spirituality, professionalism, intellectualism and traditionalism. It can
be easily identified by its conversation: "I will not! I didn't! It's your fault!
You said ... You did ... You are ...!" The results are seen in the backwash
of broken homes and maladjusted personalities. It is evident in
psychosomatic illnesses, functional nervous disorders, chronic
unhappiness and anxiety. It is apparent in interpersonal stresses,
domestic and vocational traumas, financial bondage and more. Surely
this is not our desire. Neither is this our Lord's design. This was made
obvious when Jesus asserted:

"I am come that they might have life and that they might have it more abundantly." - John 10:10

Eternal life comes by faith, and only by faith in the sacrifice Jesus wrought on Calvary. Abundant living, however, does not come by faith.

It is ours by obedience. Abundant living is our rightful inheritance. Our heritage is to enjoy life in its fullest dimension. The key is obedience. Obey the principles for victorious living and then you will enjoy the abundance.

The first place to start is to lay an axe to the trunk of pride. When this tree is cut down at the roots, all the unwanted symptoms of social sickness will begin to drop off like dying leaves! Here is how to do it:

1. Obey the words of Ephesians 5:21:

    "Submitting yourselves one to another in the fear of God!"

2. Submit yourself to the wise counsel of Proverbs 12:15:

    "The way of a fool is right in his own eyes: but he that hearkeneth unto counsel is wise!"

3. Treat others with preferential care according to Romans 12:10:

    "Be kindly affectioned one to another with brotherly love; in honour preferring one another!"

4. Act in every way which is pleasing to God, in agreement with Colossians 3:17:

    "And whatsoever ye do in word or deed, do all in the name of the Lord Jesus, giving thanks to God and the Father by him! "

This is one key to successful living!

KEY 18 SKELETONS IN YOUR CLOSET

Past experiences hold an inexorable power over our everyday lives. Experiences are the seeds which germinate and grow into a veritable garden of values, ideals, goals, tastes, customs, habits, convictions, aspirations, preferences, modus operandi, abilities, traits and knowledge. These are some of the dynamics which make you who you really are. They are programmed into your thinking during the developmental years or accepted as concepts during adulthood. It is a well-known fact that we become what we have experienced.

War creates many traumatic experiences. The memory of exploding bombs, fire and the whine of sirens, the loss of loved-ones, the smell of burning flesh and dismembered bodies, leaves impressions that take decades to heal. The common term *shell-shock* was used to describe people who became dysfunctional as a result of such traumas. Failure and social rejection create uncertainty and doubt about your own value. Positive approval, social acceptance and notable achievements, on the other hand, generate self-assurance and confidence. Wise choices are based upon correct information, but misinformation or disinformation can only lead to disaster. In a very real sense, you are what you have experienced. This is the reason for the fruits you display in your life.

One of the sad realities of modern society is that much of our programming is faulty. Radio, television, the news media, the lyrics of modern music and the educational system are the leading culprits in the dissemination of misinformation. Home and family relationships, however, can inflict the greatest harm, or provide the greatest benefit. Malachi, the last of the Old Testament prophets, records an interesting warning:

"Behold, I will send you Elijah the prophet before the coming of the great and dreadful day of the Lord: And he shall turn the heart of the fathers to the children, and the heart of the children to their fathers, lest I come and smite the earth with a curse." - *Malachi 4:5-6*

We have produced a generation of fatherless children. Every child has been sired, but pitifully few have been fathered. Seventy two percent of all our children in school today, come from broken homes, single parent homes or the home of a stepparent. Few children know what it is to be held and loved by their fathers. Few have ever felt approval, acceptance or been made to feel important. Think of the emotional and mental scarring that occurs. Our only hope is to have the home and family values restored to God's original intent.

The problem does not stop here either. Even in homes where the natural parents are present, many children suffer the same treatment, as absentee fathers seek to build an empire or make ends meet. Furthermore, a misinformed or maladjusted parent will inflict his maladjustment on the entire household. This is apparent from the values which are taught. For example, our self-value is usually based upon performance. This is evidenced by such well-known statements as: "Johnny, be a good boy and mow the lawn! Sue, would you please clean up the kitchen like a good girl! Study hard and bring home an A on your report card like a good student! Don't be a dope! You can do better than that!" This kind of programming teaches us that our value is directly related to how well we are able to perform. The only logical conclusion we can arrive at is: "If I perform well, then I am good!" If my behaviour is under-par, then I am something less than good. And should my behaviour be disappointing or shameful, then I am no good;

horrible, dreadful, deplorable and every other synonym which may describe failure. This kind of mind-set leads to three natural responses.

1. SELF-CONDEMNATION

Here a person evaluates his own performance against the grid-work of past programming and finds it lacking. He concludes that it falls far short of minimum standards and is "not good." Honest evaluation gives way to self-criticism. This is evidenced by such statements or feelings as: "I'm no good! I just can't! I wish I could be like my friend! If I was only a bit better! Please excuse me, I'm such a klutz! There is no use in trying! I give up!" Such conclusions result in a severe devaluation of personal worth. It offers little pleasure or hope.

2. SELF-ABASEMENT

Punishment is the usual reward for poor performance. When we were children, our parents did this for us. As adults, it would be unnatural to paddle ourselves with a switch. After all, what would others think if they saw me "beating my own bottom" with a wooden spoon? Such a person would certainly qualify as a case study for a paper on "Abnormal Psychology and Contemporary Life". Since this kind of reward is unacceptable, we do the next best thing in order to inflict self-punishment. We simply weave a whip of guilt and flail ourselves with self-abasement. The catch- phrase goes something like this: "You should be exposed! You don't deserve anything better! You better pray to God that you are never discovered! You should be tied to a pole and flogged! You are guilty, aren't you? You sure blew it!" Since everyone is watching, you determine never to show your face in public again. This response only exacerbates the condition.

3. WITHDRAWAL AND ISOLATION

The next response is to hide. Why run the risk of exposure? The tendency is to withdraw from competitive relationships. These are some of the thoughts which occupy the reclusive mind: "If I get involved, others may see me for who I really am. Once they catch on, they will reject me." Such rejection would be crushing. To avoid this risk, we seek to avoid every circumstance where such exposure may be possible. "After all," said one man, "it is better to let some people think that I am stupid, than to get involved and dissolve any doubt they might have had!"

An astute lady from a fine upstanding church confessed: "I have frequently contemplated suicide. I genuinely hate myself. I have a hard time sleeping. I am unable to accept any love that my husband or children or anyone give me. I feel dirty most of the time!" She had a deep love for her husband and children and knew that everyone loved and respected her. Yet she was bound by deep feelings of self-abasement.

During therapy it was discovered that her problem began when she was a student in college. To pay for her tuition she took employment as a high class "escort". "I was nothing more than a common prostitute!" she sobbed. Although this incident took place some twenty years earlier, the guilt hung over her like an evil monster. She was fearful that someone, someday, somewhere at some point would discover her sordid past. Her tormenting fear became her punishment. It developed into an emotional cancer which sapped her energy, joy and productivity. A better reaction is to take a definite action to correct the problem. This she did, and was set free from her obsession.

Do you have a skeleton in some dark closet? There is no need to keep it there. It is time to do some spring-cleaning. Make a quality decision to do something about it and take decisive action. Rid yourself of the old unsightly bones. They serve no purpose. They only occupy needed space and rattle around in the chambers of your memories. This was the testimony of Paul, the Apostle:

"But this one thing I do, forgetting those things which are behind, and reaching forth unto those things which are before, I press toward the mark for the prize of the high calling of God in Christ Jesus." - *Philippians 3:13-14*

Here are some helpful thoughts which can assist you in spring- cleaning your mental closet.

1. Closet storage of skeletons is not unique. It is a common and universal problem. Most people have memories they would rather forget. Take some comfort in the fact that you are in broad company.

2. The unpleasant events of the past exist only as thoughts in your memory. They have no bearing on the present. They can only affect the present when you preoccupy your mind with past images. They can impair only as much as you allow.

3. Memories can be liars. Reality is never as we remember it. Sweet nostalgia can add to a memory, while terror can delete, and visa versa. It is highly probable that things were not as bad as you remember them.

4. Accept God's forgiveness. Forgive yourself! Suppose the events of the past were really as horrendous as you remember them to be, must you be chained to them for the rest of your life? Is there no forgiveness or release? Certainly there is. You may have been a big sinner, but Jesus Christ is a bigger Saviour! There is no past so sordid, so traumatic, so regrettable that forgiveness and cleansing cannot be found. There is an answer for every guilty memory. This is the import of 1 John 1:8-9:

> *"If we say we have no sin, we deceive ourselves, and the truth is not in us. If we confess our sins, He is faithful and just to forgive us our sins, and to cleanse us from all unrighteousness."*

Have you ever wondered whatever became of the old whore? The reference is to Rahab, the lady of ill-repute on the walls of Jericho. The Bible identifies her as "the harlot". Her story can be found in the sixth chapter of Joshua. A harlot is a prostitute, a whore. A whore of eighty years of age is an old whore. We know her story when she was young, but what ever happened to her? Her story is most exhilarating. Single-handedly she brought her entire family into the camp of Israel, while the rest of Jericho perished. She married one of Joshua's captains by the name of Salmon (Matthew 1:5) and they gave birth to a child they named Boaz. Boaz, the kinsman redeemer who married Ruth, is a type of Jesus Christ. And Boaz sired Obed, and Obed Jesse, and Jesse David (1 Chronicles 2:11-12), the very genealogy of Jesus! Our Lord Jesus Christ has a pure spotless virgin in his lineage and also a lady of ill-repute, who was made a partaker of divine nature, pure and spotless. The book of Hebrews, chapter eleven, records the names of great patriarchs. Abel, Enoch, Noah and Abraham are listed. Two women are mentioned. One is Sara. The other is not the virgin Mary, but Rahab, the former harlot, cleansed and virgin pure!

You can take a great deal of comfort in the fact that Jesus is a greater Saviour than anyone can be a sinner. You can also feel secure in the fact that your past need not be a part of your present. I once was a youth. I once was a child. Before that I was a fetus in my mother's womb. I am not a child now! In a similar way, I can declare that I once was a sinner. I once was a sinner saved by grace. Today, I am a citizen of Heaven, a child of the King, the very temple of God! Because I have been made a partaker of divine nature, I have everything I need for life and Godliness through my knowledge of Him. (2 Peter 12:3-4) This is a liberating reality for every Christian.

5. Choose to forget your unpleasant past. There are only two parties who remember your painful history. The first is you. The second is the Devil who wont let you forget. He is called the accuser of the brethren and he gets a great deal of macabre delight from your misery. God does not remember your iniquities. He has buried them in the depths of his forgetfulness, and will remember them against you no more. Once you confess your past to Him, He forgives you and promptly forgets. Not that God is incapable of remembering, but He makes a quality decision to **forget** ! When Satan goes before God's throne to accuse you, God replies, "I forgave him/her because of my Son's blood sacrifice, and I distinctly remember forgetting that past!" It would be God-like for you to do the same.

6. Accept yourself as an equal among equals. Your life has purpose and meaning. Your past experiences have served as a training period in preparation for ministry to others. It serves to qualify you to be an

understanding help to others who need you. This fact is underscored by the encouraging words of 2 Corinthians 1:3-4:

"Blessed be God, even the Father of our Lord Jesus Christ, the Father of mercies, and the God of all comfort; who comforteth us in all our tribulation, that we may be able to comfort them which are in any trouble, by the comfort wherewith we ourselves are comforted of God."

7. Be happy with **you**! Enjoy the **now**! Don't even look at the old bones. They should be buried out of sight. Remember the old cliche, **out of sight, out of mind**. In this case, it works.

8. Say this prayer with me. Aloud, so your ears can hear the confession of your mouth, pray:

"Dear Lord, I confess that my past experiences have affected my attitude, my emotions and my performance. Erase their effect on my life by forgiving me and cleansing me. Set me free to enjoy the life for which I was created. You have made me this promise, which I now receive. Thank you for honouring my request. I pray this prayer in the name of your Son Jesus. Amen."

9. Make this declaration with me: "I'm free as a bird let out of a snare! I'm free of every bondage! I'm happy I'm me! This is a great day and I shall enjoy its every moment!"

10. Live with confidence. When your conscience is clear of guilt and condemnation, then you can walk in victory and success. Meditate on the declaration of 1 John 3:20-21:

"For if our heart condemn us, God is greater than our heart, and knoweth all things. Beloved, if our heart condemn us not, then have we confidence toward God."

This is one key to successful living!

KEY 19 EXPOSURE TO A SICK SOCIETY

Too much *Fun in the Sun* can be dangerous to your health. Sunbathers are warned that prolonged exposure to the sun can cause skin cancer. In much the same way, too much exposure to a sick society can lead to melanoma of the soul. In his book titled *Abnormal Psychology And Modern Life*, Professor of Psychology at the University of California at Los Angeles, James C Coleman, makes the following statement on page two:

"The seventeenth century has been called the Age of Enlightenment; the eighteenth, the Age of Reason; the nineteenth, the Age of Progress; and the twentieth, **the age of anxiety.**"

Behavioral scientists generally agree that ours is a "**sick society**". Whether we agree with this assessment or not, we must acknowledge that functional nervous disorders and personality maladjustment are wide spread. The factors which contribute to a person's debilitating, besetting problems are many, but the leading factor is our excessive exposure to the sick society in which we live. It all looks natural and innocent, this world in which we live, but do not be deceived by its benign subtlety. The Environmental Protection Agency posts this warning label on most social events: "Toxic, hazardous to your health!"

Exposure to a sick society

In a TV commercial, a well known sports figure interviews several people by asking, "How do you spell **relief?**" The programmed answer is always the same: "Why, I spell relief, R-O-L-A-I-D-S!" Viewers were subjected to this intensive promotional onslaught for months. Some time later, after the advertising campaign had ceased, a survey was conducted among grade three children. Among the questions which they were asked was this thought-provoking query: "How do you spell relief?" You guessed it! It was reported that eighty-five percent spelled relief, "R-O-L-A-I-D-S!" The conditioning process was complete. When these children grow up and acid indigestion strikes, which it surely will, where do you suppose they will go to find **relief?**

The influence which the outside world exerts on our thinking and behaviour is enormous. It is for this reason that more money is spent on advertising than on our national defense. The average housewife in North America sees more than five-hundred commercials a month! She has learned how to squeeze toilet paper with an enthusiastic smile; she is not ashamed to talk about such personal problems as constipation or bladder control; and she loses twenty-five pounds (12 kg) every time she dons certain undergarments. Absurd? Not at all! Manufacturers and advertising companies know full well that when your need arises, your money will make their registers ring with your hard earned cash.

Man's thought and behavioral patterns are conditioned by the input he receives. So widely is this fact accepted that a well-known cliche was born: **garbage in, garbage out.** The information you receive through your senses, is the information which forms the foundation upon which your life-style is built, be it garbage or precious metals. It must be remembered that all behaviour is determined by choice, and choice is based upon the information you possess. It matters not whether the information is accurate or spurious, your decisions are determined by it. It is easily seen how false information can lead to tragic choices. If a buyer could be convinced that product "A" is better than product "B", it is product "A" that will be purchased. Con-artists are skilled in bilking people out of their life's earnings, by gaining their confidence and persuading them to make fatal choices.

The problem modern man faces is that he has become thoroughly homogenized with his **sick society**. Daytime soap operas, the world of entertainment, a biased educational system, faulty instruction, partial justice, brutal law enforcement, political corruption, famines and epidemics, economic pressures, discrimination, violence, "My friend, Jake", and a host of other forces seek to impose their values upon us. These clarion voices cry out that infidelity is fine, immorality is acceptable, perversion is vogue, graft is groovie, brutality is understandable, violence is exciting, lawlessness is good business sense and that the end always justifies the means. Furthermore, any attempt to resist this spreading contagion, is scoffed at as being archaic. This scenario is unpleasant, if not offensive, but it is factual.

In the book of Revelation, John writes to the seven churches in Asia. The church at Pergamos (312 - 606 AD), as described in Revelation 2:12-16, became a Roman possession in 133 AD. It was the capital of Mysia, about 20 miles (32 km) from the sea. It was an illustrious city, renowned for its wealth, fashion and religion. Known for its many religions, the residents were called "The Temple Keepers." This was one of the cities which vied for the privilege of worshipping the Emperor. The Christian church so indulged in the affairs of this modern city that they became indistinguishable from anyone else. They had placed their trust in Jesus Christ as their Lord and Saviour, yet looked, acted, and smelled like everyone else. They were thoroughly homogenized with their culture. It is interesting to note that the name, Pergamos, means "Thoroughly Married!"

It must be noted that modern society, with its agencies and institutions, influences our lives positively as well. This is a great period of history in which to live. Be encouraged, but be a **discriminating participant** in the society in which you live. There are times you are called upon to be a protestant. This is the import of 1 Thessalonians 5:22: "... *abstain from all appearance of evil.*"

If it looks bad, stay away!

Unfortunately, modern man has developed a bad habit of looking at, tasting, feeling, smelling and ingesting that which is destructive to him. If you are caught up in society's value systems, mind-sets and modes of operating, you are likely to experience much of the world's neurosis. This will include such harmful consequences as depression, worry, fear, anxiety, disillusionment, hopelessness and a host of emotional reactions. The somatic responses to these can be overwhelming. The check list is surprisingly long and includes many familiar effects. Mark those you have experienced:

Migraine headaches
Hyperventilation
Heart palpitations
Ulcerated stomachs
Skin rashes
Muscle spasms
Allergies
Asthma
Arthritis
Spastic colon
Respiratory ailments
Insomnia
Hypertension
Fatigue
Compulsive eating
Excessive drinking
Fingernail biting
Nervousness
Exhaustion
Listlessness
Weariness
Nightmares

This list is not nearly complete, but it does give an idea of how directly our society influences us. The degree to which you experience negative or harmful emotions, is directly proportionate to your exposure to destructive concepts. God has given us His prescription for an effective cure against such disorders:

"This is what the Lord says: Cursed is the one who trusts in man, who depends on flesh for his strength and whose heart turns away from the Lord. He will be like a bush in the wastelands; he will not see prosperity when it comes. He will dwell in the parched places of the desert, in a salt land where no one lives. But blessed is the man who trusts in the Lord, whose confidence is in Him. He will be like a tree planted by the water that sends out its roots by the stream. It does not fear when heat comes; its leaves are always green. It has no worries in a year of drought and never fails to bear fruit." - Jeremiah 17:5-8 (New International Version)

That's for me! For a life of carefree success, I will expose my mind to God's precepts, to His concepts. I encourage you to draw the same conclusion for your life.

This is one key to successful living!

KEY 20   NOT CURE BUT DELIVERANCE

Is it cure or deliverance that we need to be set free from the clutches of a sick society? The word **cure** comes from a French and Latin word *cura* which means to restore to health; to bring about recovery; to rectify. The word suggests a prescription or a course of action which facilitates healing. If the causative factors for ill health can be discovered and removed, the human body will heal itself.

1. CURE

The process for cure is a standard procedure, which moves from analysis through diagnosis, deduction, prescription, and cure, to health.

1.1 Analysis

All the symptoms and contingencies must be gathered and carefully analyzed. The following scenario is a case in point. A patient comes to his doctor with an assortment of pin-like punctures randomly displayed on his gluteus maxims, the large muscle of the buttocks. Upon careful scrutiny, it is learned that there are no pincushions or sharp projectiles in his work environment and that no contact had been made with a porcupine or like creature. However, the patient's wife has a love for cactus plants and grows them for a hobby.

1.2 Diagnosis

The relationship between the symptoms and all contingencies must be established. Example: It is discovered that one cactus in particular, has spines that exactly match the punctures in question, that the lady of the house had placed that specific plant on the recliner in the sunlight, and that the husband came home from the office early for a needed rest.

1. 3 Deduction

The actual cause and effect relationship between the symptoms and the contingencies must be determined. Example: Upon further examination, a direct relationship between the cactus plant and the patient's posterior is established. The patient, unaware of his wife's actions, threw himself on the recliner for his needed rest, but he didn't recline, neither did he get his needed rest!

1.4 Prescription

The plan is to restore the patient to health by altering the relationship between the cause and effect factors. A correct prescription would read something like this:

"Take two aspirin, drink lots of water, get to bed early, and avoid sitting on the cactus!"

A person need not be a mental giant to know that this prescription will cure the paling impaled patient. The cure is often a simple procedure: "Get off the cacti!"

1.5 Cure

In the course of time, the assorted pin-like punctures will disappear. The result will be recovered health. Few of the problems we face in life are as bizarre as this, but all follow the same basic process for cure. If the cause for the problem can be determined, its removal can lead to cure. However, cure cannot always be that simple.

There are many obstacles which can prevent cure. First, the cause cannot always be determined. Second, if the cause can be confirmed, it is not always certain what can be done about it. Third, if certainty can be established, it is not always true that time, money, ability or technology will permit cure. There are many who face such a dilemma. In such a case, it is not **cure** that is needed, but **deliverance** .

2. DELIVERANCE

Deliverance comes from two French words *de* + *liberare* meaning to rescue away from; to liberate from; to bring deliverance. It implies that the one being delivered is incapable of self-help or cure. Such a person is much like the historical character, Lazarus, who had died and had been entombed four days. There was nothing he could do about his condition. He was beyond cure. Only deliverance could set him free. The narrative is found in John 11:43-44:

> *"And when He (Jesus) thus had spoken, he cried with a loud voice, Lazarus, come forth. And he that was dead came forth, bound hand and foot with grave-clothes: and his face was bound about with a napkin. Jesus saith unto them (those of his friends and family who were present),* **loose him, and let him go.***"*

The dynamics for deliverance follow the same procedure as for cure, except for the last step: analysis, diagnosis, deduction, prescription, and then deliverance. Deliverance presupposes two things. First: There are those who are willing to take the time, effort and personal responsibility to set the captive free. Second: The one in bondage is willing to accept the attempts made on his behalf. Here is a list of several common situations from which we need deliverance.

2.1 Personal problems

As in the case of Lazarus, those who are bound by personal problems can be "loosed" by qualified guidance and counselling. Functional nervous disorders, emotional traumas and interpersonal or domestic conflicts can be "cut off", just like so many grave clothes. Proverbs 11:14 states: *"Where no counsel is, the people fall."*

2.2 Individual ignorance

Those who lack information or receive misinformation can be "liberated" by sound instruction. It stands to reason that if I am lost in a city, correct direction can get me to my destination. For this reason many world governments operate a Bureau of Disinformation which is responsible for disseminating misinformation. The sole purpose for these lies is to confuse the enemy. The teaching of values, morals, ethics and other foundational truths, is the responsibility of the parents and is vital for successful living. Children who lack such instruction are ill-prepared to avoid bondage. John 8:32 declares:

"Ye shall know the truth, and the truth shall make you free."

2.3 Financial indebtedness

Those who are bound by debt, can be loosed by financial planning. Indebtedness is a leading cause for marital breakdown. Worries over money is a major cause for emotional dysfunction. Proverbs 22:7 asserts that: *"The borrower is servant to the lender."* The slavery of indebtedness can be broken by budget control, income and expenditure discipline, vocational opportunities, sound investment, priority evaluation, encouragement and financial aid. Welfare is not the government's responsibility. It belongs to the family and the church. Isaiah made this clear in chapter 58.

2.4 Personal loneliness

Those who find themselves exiled to a life of loneliness can be set free by the interaction of friends. Reach out and touch someone with your love. In order to win some friends, you must be winsome. 1 Timothy 3:2 tells us to be *"... given to hospitality."*

2.5 Personal blindness

Those who find themselves in spiritual darkness, unable to sense the power and presence of God, can be "loosed" by divine grace. This is a spiritual experience called "salvation". Jesus makes this life-changing offer in John 10:10 "*I am come that you might have life, and have it more abundantly.*" Pray this simple prayer: "Dear Lord Jesus. Save me! Forgive me of my sins. Take away my blindness and give me sight to see You as my Deliverer and my Saviour. I invite You to come into my heart. Share your life with me. I receive your deliverance this day. I ask this in Your Name, Jesus. Amen."

2.6 Inopportunity

Those who have not had the *lucky breaks*, can be *set free* from the *old salt mines* by opportunity and possibility. Proverbs 18:16 makes it clear that: "*A man's gift maketh room for him.*" In simple terms, a man's natural ability is God's gift to him. It was given to provide a livelihood and a sense of fulfilment for him. Whether it be educational advancement, specialized training, vocational opportunities or service ministries, a person can develop his talents for a purpose and for personal satisfaction.

2.7 Rebellion

Many people are bound by obstinate rebellion. This is displayed by an attitude which says, "I will not listen! You can't tell me what to do! Don't cramp my style! We shall do it my way! I am right! I'll have it my way!" and other statements of exaggerated independence. Rebellion is so offensive to God that He calls it "witchcraft"! A person who does not have a teachable spirit is in rebellion. Repentance is the only means of deliverance. The word repentance comes from two Greek words *meta* meaning to join up with, and *kneehow* meaning knowledge. It means to join ourselves with the knowledge of God. This is true deliverance! You can be set free, if you want to. You can also be the instrument of someone else's freedom.

This is one key for successful living!

KEY 21   WHO IN THE WORLD AM I?

If you were placed in a police line-up with ten other people, could you point out which one is you? If ten photographs of nine other people plus yourself were set before you, could you pick out your picture? The answer is obvious - certainly! If, however, the personality profiles of ten people were placed on your table, could you identify which one is yours? Could you identify yourself? It is doubtful.

We usually think of ourselves in terms of physical features, but a person is infinitely more than just a body. Man is so earth-oriented that he believes life is limited to physical realities. We are essentially *Spirit Beings,* who possess a *Soul* and live in a container called the *Body!* Set aside your temporal body and your eternal spirit for a moment, and focus your attention upon your soul.

The Bible uses the Greek word *Psuche* to describe your immaterial nature. It is translated as *Mind* in Romans 12:1-2 and Philippians 2:5, and *Soul* in 3 John 2. The English words psychology, psychiatry and psychometry are derived from it. It identifies the sum total of who you are. It refers to your person and personality. During the evening service one Sunday, a newly converted man stood to his feet to give his testimony:

"I woke up this morning, looked in the mirror, and said, Who in the world am I?"

The audience broke into snorts, giggles and audible laughter. The man's question, however, had a great deal of depth and meaning. Who are you? If you were not permitted to use a physical description, how would you describe yourself?

There are a number of instruments available which will give an accurate diagrammatical representation of your physical characteristics. The X-ray, camera, video and mirror are but a few. Everyone is able to recognize his image in a picture or a mirror. Most people spend many hours looking at a mirror in the hope of improving their outward appearance. One reason why people spend so little time improving the inward person, is because they have never seen themselves as they really are. Here is a psychological mirror that will give you a subjective image of your personality and character. It will reflect your image in fifty different areas, ranging from one extreme to the other.

You will find the exercise interesting and revealing. The instructions are easy to follow. Listed are fifty sets of characteristics. Each characteristic stands opposite in nature to the other, as cold does to hot, tall is to short and fast is to slow. Read the brief description of each characteristic and determine which one describes you most accurately. Once this has been done, determine the degree or the intensity to which you function in this capacity: average, moderate or excessive. Please note that 1 and 5 are both **excessive** intensities, but in opposite characteristics. The same is also true for 2 and 4, which are both **moderate** degrees, in opposing qualities. An **average** response is 3. This is true for each trait.

Excessive - 1;   Moderate - 2;   Average - 3;   Moderate - 4;   and Excessive - 5.

Evaluate your behaviour, attitudes and emotions and place a check mark at the number which best describes you. For example: If you are excessively **reserved**: reclusive; would rather work with objects and things than be with people; withdrawn and non-communicative, you would score yourself: 1- Excessive, 2 - Moderate, or 3 - Average. On the other hand, you may see yourself as **outgoing**: on the move; seldom at home; the life of the party; you would have been happier if you had been born with wheels instead of feet, then you would evaluate yourself: 5 - Excessive, 4 - Moderate, or 3 - Average. Use this same method to the end of the evaluation. None of the characteristics are good or bad. They are different from each other. You need not be intimidated by this evaluation, simply because you can neither pass nor fail.

Because of the subjective nature of self-analysis, it is difficult to be accurate. Self-deception is a powerful force. Please be objective in your answers. Be honest with yourself. Don't be afraid to see yourself. Unpleasant characteristics can be changed as easily as an unpleasant hairdo. This is the instruction of Romans 12:3:

"For by the grace given me I say to every one of you: Do not think of yourself more highly than you ought, but rather think of yourself with sober judgment, in accordance with the measure of faith God has given you." (New International Version)

Who is this reflection in my psychological mirror?

Excessive 1; Moderate 2; Average 3; Moderate 4; Excessive 5.

Reserved   1 2 3 4 5   **Outgoing**

A reserved person is aloof, shy, quiet and withdrawn. He would choose a work place by himself and enjoy his own company. He carefully avoids groups of people.

The outgoing person is gregarious, extroverted and on the move. He enjoys people and seeks to be the life of the party. The engine in his car seldom gets cold!

Concrete   1 2 3 4 5   **Abstract**

A concrete person is factual, tangible and mechanical. He prefers to work with objects and things. He is adept at working with his hands: fixing, making and erecting.

The abstract person is theoretical. He likes discussions about politics, religion and philosophy. He frequents the art gallery and the library, and enjoys the opera.

Ambivalent   1 2 3 4 5   **Stable**

An ambivalent person is uncertain, doubtful and undulating. Choices are based upon vacillating variables. Decisions are made, then remade. He is like a moving target.

The stable individual is constant, sure and secure. This person is seldom moved by persuasion, emotion, reversals or set-backs. Can be hard and unyielding.

Accommodating   1 2 3 4 5   **Assertive**

The accommodating person is obliging, serving and indulging. He seeks to serve others and is therefore liked by those around him. He seldom rocks the boat.

An assertive person is forward, domineering and outspoken. He often gets his way. He conducts himself as foreman of the job, and assumes leadership.

Sedate   1 2 3 4 5   **Enthusiastic**

A sedate person is non-excitable. He is sombre, grave and imperturbable. His emotional mood-swings are undetectable. Can be viewed as unfeeling and unsympathetic.

The enthusiastic person is highly spirited, zealous and effervescent. He walks with a bounce in his step and life is a joy. Problems are seen as stepping stones to success.

Timid   1   2   3   4   5   **Bold**

A timid person is fainthearted and shy. He sees life as a series of uncertainties which must be reality-tested. He lacks confidence and is fearful of trying anything different.

The bold person is fearless, forward and daring. He is not afraid to try anything once. His forays can leave him out on the limb. He can be misinterpreted as reckless.

Tough   1   2   3   4   5   **Sensitive**

A tough-minded person is hard, callous and unyielding. His choices are firm and factual. He is intransigence, unforgiving, does well in business, but lacks domestic acumen.

The sensitive person is responsive, compassionate and feeling. He relates well with people, is understanding and nurturing. Others may take advantage of his kindness.

Trusting   1   2   3   4   5   **Suspicious**

The trusting person is believing and accepting. He avoids judgmental attitudes and seeks to identify with others. He may be misinterpreted as being gullible.

A suspicious person is sceptical and distrustful. He does not listen to what people say but rather wonders why. He is always trying to out-guess others and to gain the upper-hand.

Practical   1 2 3 4 5   **Imaginative**

A practical person is pragmatic and realistic. He is governed by external realities. His concern is efficiency, time-management and quality control.

The imaginative person is innovative and creative. Colours, forms and lines are important and he likes to try new and different things, even at the expense of convenience.

Unpretentious   1 2 3 4 5   **Flamboyant**

The unpretentious person is modest, unassuming and plain. He is not concerned about polish, poise or flare. He is genuine and does not put on airs.

A flamboyant individual is polished, orchestrated, programmed and excessively flashy. His flare can be seen as theatrics.

Confident   1 2 3 4 5   **Apprehensive**

A confident person is assured and certain. He trusts in his own abilities. He is willing to step out into a venture and to suffer the consequences and enjoy the rewards.

The apprehensive person is fearful, wary and uneasy. He is concerned about the uncertainties and contingencies, and will not risk present security for a future potential.

Conservative   1 2 3 4 5   **Liberal**

The conservative person observes traditional values. He is orthodox and respects established principles. He is a person of substance and meaning. His word is his honour.

A liberal person is unconventional and is not confined to restricted thinking. He is willing to try a different approach. He is permissive, accepting and free-thinking.

Group-dependent   **1   2   3   4   5**   **Self-trusting**

A group-dependent individual is acquiescent and reliant. He needs the approval and applause of others to ensure his value. He is easily led by peer pressure.

The self-trusting person is adequate in himself and is self-sufficient. He is competent and is willing to stand alone in a crowd. He is a trend-setter.

Undisciplined   **1   2   3   4   5**   **Controlled**

An undisciplined person has difficulty in following through or finishing a project. He is unreliable and irresponsible. He lives according to his urges.

The controlled individual is composed and collected. Convenience takes a second place to the project. He is detailed and responsible.

Relaxed   **1   2   3   4   5**   **Tense**

The relaxed person is tranquil, calm and at ease. Problems do not seem to bother him and he takes things in his stride. He is undisturbed by disturbances.

A tense person is anxious, troubled and overwrought. He sees a small problem as an horrendous setback. He can be easily agitated. He is up-tight and can be reactionary.

Happy   **1   2   3   4   5**   **Burdened**

A happy person is cheerful, joyful and easily delighted. He chooses to see the good and enjoys living. Few things seem to burden him. He is good-natured and laughs readily.

The burdened person is encumbered, weighted down with concerns. He appears oppressed, as though preoccupied with overwhelming responsibilities. He is in a cloud of gloom.

Contented   1   2   3   4   5   **Dissatisfied**

Contented people make better neighbours, friends and family members. They are satisfied, gratified and grateful people. They are thankful for the little things.

A dissatisfied person is seldom content. Little things are an irritation to him. He constantly looks for more. When expectation is not forthcoming, he is aggravated.

Cautious   1   2   3   4   5   **Adventurous**

A cautious person does not take chances. He is pondering, deliberate and careful. The end-result must be assured before a commitment is made.

The adventurous person is experimenting. He is exploring the new, ever living beyond the comfort zone. Change is sheer serendipity.

Calm   1   2   3   4   5   **Excitable**

The calm individual is composed, cool and collected. He appears satisfied with his state and is in control of its outcome. He seldom becomes rattled.

An excitable person is temperamental and hypersensitive. He easily becomes elated with fortune and swings to depression when things go wrong. He can be reactionary.

Enthusiastic   1   2   3   4   5   **Wearied**

Enthusiastic people are spirited, ardent and positive. They are confident and self-motivated. They seek to make things happen.

A wearied person watches things happen. He is fatigued and drained. He appears exhausted and lacking in interest. He sees life as heavy and burdensome.

Guilt-free   1   2   3   4   5   **Guilt-prone**

A guilt-free person does not accept blame or fault. He rejects any notion that he may be the cause of problems. He may give way to projection, denial or rationalization.

The guilt-prone individual accepts all guilt and blame. Everything is his fault: world famine, ozone depletion, environmental pollution, and the prime lending rate.

Moralistic   1   2   3   4   5   **Unethical**

The moralistic person is highly principled and ethical. He can be counted upon to carry through his commitment. He can tend to be legalistic and judgmental.

An unethical person is unprincipled, and is governed by expediency. Much of what he does and says may be improper or inappropriate.

Warm   1   2   3   4   5   **Distant**

Warm people are cordial and congenial. They are personal, approachable and touchable. They relate well with others and make a meaningful contribution to their lives.

A distant person is aloof, detached and impersonal. He can appear to be cold and metallic. He is lacking in feeling, sympathy and empathy.

Amiable   1   2   3   4   5   **Overbearing**

The amiable person is likeable. He makes a pleasant companion. He is warm, he accepts others, and he willingly cooperates. He doesn't rock the boat.

An overbearing individual is domineering, bossy and must have his way. He is pushy and must be in charge. He is demanding and controlling.

Positive	1 2 3 4 5	**Poor**
Self-image		**Self-image**

People who have a positive self-image know who they are and what their calling is. They have a sense of destiny and have achieved a measure of success.

People who have a poor self-image feel inadequate and inferior. They often have feelings of rejection and failure, and can point to few successes.

After evaluating yourself, it may be interesting to see how your spouse sees you! Would others see you as you see yourself? This evaluation will do one of two things. It will either open the doors of communication and understanding, or it will lead to the breaking of dishes and furniture in your home! The mature individual will see this as an opportunity to gain a new understanding of self and of others, rather than of serving as a point of contention. It will answer your question: "Who in the world am I?"

This is one key to successful living!

KEY 22   HOW TO CONQUER DEPRESSION

"I cry a lot. I can't sleep at nights. I have no appetite. I am unhappy most of the time. Nothing seems to interest me any more. My happiest times are when I am mildly depressed. The rest of the time I am super-depressed. I feel like that forlorn hill-billy who moaned, 'If I had no bad luck, I'd have no luck at all!'" These were the exact words of one person who had come to my office for counselling. Clinical records clearly show that these are the true feelings of countless people. A depressed emotional state incapacitates more people than all other health problems combined. More than half of all hospital beds are occupied by people suffering from emotional problems. The results of depression can be very incapacitating.

1. THE EFFECTS OF DEPRESSION

Depression has become our nation's number one health problem. The results range from functional nervous disorders to abnormal behaviour. A depressive state often follows a stressful circumstance. It is characterized by abnormally excessive sadness. This may last for long periods of time, but will eventually dissipate and return to a normal state. Webster's Dictionary defines depression as: "The act of depressing; abasement; dejection ... a weakening of vitality."

Depression produces many harmful consequences. Here are several common effects. If you are experiencing any of these, you may be mildly depressed.

1.1 Depression restricts happiness

The joy of living is lost. Every hour of the day is poisoned with unhappiness and feelings of futility. Life is reduced to a tedious existence. The whole thing seems pointless! A morbid dejection characterizes each moment.

1.2 Depression reduces creativity and productivity

Accomplishments become marginal at best. Work backlogs and the tasks of daily routine become overwhelming as chores never get done. Even worse, there is that pervasive and ever gnawing feeling that it will never change. There is no better way of living; why try?

1. 3 Depression distorts the view of reality

With depression comes a gross misinterpretation of what reality is like and what it should be. When perceptions become inaccurate, little problems become major obstacles, minor reversals become tragic setbacks, and trite irritations become excruciatingly painful. Whether serious or insignificant, the "victim" becomes overwhelmed with the enormity of the task.

1.4 Depression affects the body

The term "Psycho-somatic disorders" comes from two Greek words: *psuchi* meaning soul or mind, and *soma* meaning body. Behavioral scientists have long known that biological functions are closely related to the emotional state. Emotions are dynamics of the soul or *psuchi* (better known as psyche). When destructive emotions such as anger, hate, bitterness, anxiety or depression are chronically entertained, they harmfully affect the body or *soma*. Hence, a physical ailment which is caused by an emotional state is called a **psycho-somatic** disorder.

Psycho-somatic disorders are biological problems which have no organic causes. They are caused solely by unresolved emotional stresses. In simple terms: **you don't get ulcers from what you eat, you get ulcers from what's eating you!**

2. THE CURE FOR DEPRESSION

Is there a cure for an ambivalent emotional state such as worry, fear, anxiety, phobia and depression? Yes indeed! The best answer for its cure and prevention is surprisingly not found in medical journals or scientific research papers, nor in psychological text books. It is found in the Bible! An excellent antidote for depression is found in Philippians 4:6-7. The prescription, as set forth by the Great Physician, is as follows:

"Be careful (anxious) for nothing; but in every thing by prayer and supplication with thanksgiving let your requests be made known unto God. And the peace of God, which passeth all understanding, shall keep your hearts and minds through Christ Jesus."

2.1 Be anxious for nothing ...

The instruction here is to be careful, or full of care, for nothing. Greeks were permitted to use more than one negative in a sentence. For emphasis they could use up to three. This statement takes on a great deal of significance when we understand it in the original: *"Don't* you *never* be worried for *nothing!"* In other words, **not never no-how**! This may be poor English, but it is powerful Greek. It is also good theology and sound psychology. No problem in life is so great as to warrant the intense concern you have given it. Just don't ever worry about anything!

2.2 But in everything ...

No problem is exempt. No exceptions are allowed. Whether you struggle with an illness, a stressful marriage, a financial concern, a domestic problem, a work-related frustration or whatever, you are instructed to commit it to God. He specializes in creating order out of chaos. When you hand your problems over to God, they become His concern. You never have to worry about God's problems!

2. 3 With prayer ...

Prayer is an act of faith where we turn the welfare of our lives over to God. Man have tried it without His help. When the best of human prowess and personal efforts fail, man usually turns to Him. We are much like the World War II soldier who prayed to God while on his face in the trench. Shells were falling all around him and there were no prospects for improvement. "Oh God," he pleaded, "Please! Help me out of this mess just this once, and I'll not bother you for another twenty years!" Why wait until your world collapses?

2.4 And supplication ...

Earnest petition has a focusing effect. Problems which are ill-defined, become clearly identified. It is difficult to find a solution when the problem is not clearly understood. "Lord, you are my helper. I give the outcome of every detail to you!"

2.5 With thanksgiving ...

Ingratitude is the hallmark of the affluent. The USA has the privilege of being the richest nation in all history. Affluence, however, leads to self-indulgence. Ingratiating self-centredness seeks personal comfort. Nowhere is this more clearly seen than in our manufacturing industries. Items which sell best are those that can bring instant pleasure. America has given the world instant coffee, instant communication, instant cash, instant entertainment and world-wide travel, all in air-conditioned comfort. I like it! There is no virtue to be found in self- abasing poverty. Being grateful for it is another story. We have become so accustomed to our affluence that we take it for granted. When we are denied these comforts, we become upset. "After all," we think, "these are **my** rights! **my** needs are not being satisfied. I am happy and satisfied only when I get **my** way!"

The best therapy for those who are wrapped up in their own little subjective selves, is **thanksgiving**. Thanksgiving gets my mind off my problems and focuses my attention heavenward. I am also able to see all the world around me. Don't get so preoccupied with your problems and possible solutions that you miss all the beauty around you!

2.6 Let your requests be made known unto God ...

Tell Him about your needs. Then turn yourself and your welfare over to His tender care. The Great Physician guarantees results!

2.7 And the peace of God ...

This peace is not engineered by human prowess. It is not the result of personal intervention or manipulation. It is not a temporary fix or an emotional band-aid. It is truly a genuine supernatural peace! Therefore it is not surprising that those who trust in Him are the happiest people on earth, even in the midst of stress!

2.8 Which passes human understanding ...

This lasting peace can never be assessed by human cognition. It is a mysterious reality which is beyond human understanding. The peace that God gives is beyond personal comprehension and is overwhelming in its reality. It is far superior to that found in a therapist's office. It is also free for the asking.

2.9 Shall keep ...

The word *keep* in the original means *to fort*. The early settlers would build a *fort* to protect themselves and their possessions against the hostile enemy, beasts and inclement weather. The pioneers rested peacefully inside their fort, knowing they were safe and secure against all dangers. The import here is that **God's peace** will be the *fort* that will protect your most precious possessions: your heart and your mind.

2.10 Shall keep your hearts and minds ...

The *heart* is the seat of all human emotions. It is the well-spring from which all human feelings flow: joy, sorrow, love, hate, hope, depression, confidence, fear, enthusiasm and more. Human emotions can become tempest like a sea. The *keep* provides a safe harbour from life's storms. The *mind* is the seat of intelligence and understanding. It is the centre of cognition and choice. This *keep* provides a place of refuge for all who face uncertainty and confusion. God's peace will fortify your heart (feeler) and your mind (thinker)!

2.11 Through Christ Jesus!

The agency which cures depression is God! Human facilities are good, but they are limited in that they are partial, temporary, temperamental, intermittent and expensive. Jesus never fails. It is He who has promised, *"I will never leave thee nor forsake thee."*

This is one key to successful living!

KEY 23   THY SPEECH BETRAYS THEE

One can always tell what kind of wheels are turning in a person's head, by observing the "spokes" which keep flying out of his mouth. Thoughts profoundly affect human speech. Jesus declared that:

"Out of the abundance of the heart, the mouth speaketh." - *Matthew 12:34*

Speech is the shop-window which showcases the human mind. The vulgar-thinking person will express himself in profane, lewd and suggestive ways. His speech displays a person who struggles with self-devaluation, self-condemnation and feelings of inadequacy. Furthermore, his speech portrays a personality which has been thoroughly corrupted by the "world system". Negative thought-processes are manifested with words that reject, repudiate, disclaim, impugn and negate. Such a person wrestles with disruptive feelings. It is highly unlikely that this person will ever achieve happiness or success. Speech is self-perpetuating in that it reinforces like thinking. It also corrupts those who happen to be listening.

"Be not deceived: evil communications corrupt good manners."
- 1 Corinthians 15:33

An attractive woman in her early thirties admitted that she had few friends, could not maintain employment, was unhappy in her marriage and was as popular as a "skunk at a garden party". Her speech embarrassed other women, offended her peers and infuriated her business associates. She estranged herself from everyone who cared about her. This, in turn, embittered her because no one wished to tolerate her abrasive attitude.   When it was suggested that her relationship with others was offensive, she glared and snapped, "I will express myself as I very well please!   No one controls my mouth!" Indeed, this was true. Not even she could! The end result was evident. She became lonely, embittered and eventually sickly. She was always preoccupied with concerns regarding her "failing health". She had little left to do but to worry about her bodily functions.

It is difficult to embrace a porcupine or hug a cactus without becoming impaled. Because no one relishes the prospects of quill punctures on the chest and arms, they prudently stay away. A volume of truth is conveyed in the following poem. It graphically demonstrates the power of speech. It would do us well to commit it to memory.

> The boneless tongue so small and weak,
> can crush and kill, declared the Greek.
> The tongue destroys a greater horde,
> the Turks assert, than doth the sword.

> The Persian proverb wisely saith,
> A lengthy tongue - an early death!
> Or sometimes takes this form instead,
> Don't let your tongue cut off your head!

> The tongue can speak a word whose speed,
> Say the Chinese, outstrips the steed!
> While Arab sages this impart,
> The tongue's great storehouse is the heart!

From Hebrew hath the maxim sprung,
Though feet may slip, ne'er let the tongue!
The sacred writer crowns the whole,
Who keeps his tongue, doth keep his soul!

Like most feared predators, the tongue lives in its den. You will find it hiding behind the teeth! The warning given to us in James is simple and direct, yet no university course on *Developing Communication Skills* could be more informative.

"...the tongue is a little member, and boasteth great things. Behold, how great a matter a little fire kindleth! And the tongue is a fire, a world of iniquity: so is the tongue among our members, that it defileth the whole body, and setteth on fire the course of nature; and it is set on fire of hell. For every kind of beasts, and of birds, and of serpents, and of things in the sea, is tamed, and hath been tamed of mankind: But the tongue can no man tame; it is an unruly evil, full of deadly poison. Therewith bless we God, even the Father; and therewith curse we men, which are made after the similitude of God. Out of the same mouth proceedeth blessing and cursing. My brethren, these things ought not so to be." - *James 3:5-10*

The writer of the book of Hebrews gives us this following encouragement:

"By him therefore let us offer the sacrifice of praise to God continually, that is, the fruit of our lips giving thanks to his name. But to do good and to communicate, forget not: for with such sacrifices God is well pleased." - *Hebrews 13:15-16*

Even as your speech reflects such things as your origin, rearing, training and interests, so too does it exhibit your true nature. Your speech betrays you. An evaluation of your speech will tell you a great deal about yourself. Here are eight simple steps that will help to clean up your thinking and will, in turn, profoundly affect your speech:

1. RECOGNIZE THAT A PROBLEM EXISTS

There is no one so blind as he who refuses to see. Denial of an existing need is not only self-deceiving but also self-destroying. Like an untreated wound, it will infect healthy areas and will cause serious complications.

2. ACKNOWLEDGE THAT YOU MUST DO SOMETHING ABOUT IT

In more than thirty-five years of professional counselling, I have never had a demented person come for help. Only wise people seek counselling. Demented people are too dull to recognize that they have a problem. They stultify the process of guidance by their own indifference. Only a wise person can recognize and acknowledge that a problem exists. He may not know what to do about it. He may not be able to apply the requirements needed for change. He is wise enough, however, to recognize the problem, sufficiently motivated to do something about it, and mature enough to submit himself to the therapeutic process. This is why Solomon declares that a fool rejects instruction, but a wise man seeks counsel. (Proverbs 12:15) **Wise people still seek counsel!**

3. DETERMINE TO TAKE CORRECTIVE ACTION

Knowledge without action is inexcusable. When you fail to act upon the information you have, you choose to live in rebellion against the truth. Jesus declared that they who are justified are those who **do** the truth, not they who know it!

4. REORGANIZE YOUR PRIORITIES

Do something about the problem that is most pressing. Get started **now!** There is a tyranny in procrastination. Don't sacrifice the imperative on the altar of the important. Most of the things you do are important, but certain things are absolutely vital to life and well-being. Set aside those urgent things for the imperative. Put your priorities in order.

5. REJECT DESTRUCTIVE THINKING

Resist thoughts which say to you, "I'm no good! I can't do it! It will never change! This is my unfortunate lot in life! I'm a frump. I'm just a born loser!" This type of thinking is inconsistent with the nature of God who dwells within you.

6. REPLACE NEGATIVE THINKING PATTERNS

Thoughts and emotions are controllable, displaceable and exchangeable. Replace your negative mind-set with positive expectation. Positive thinking is scriptural. You are God's holy temple. Never disgrace His sanctuary by demeaning thinking. Ephesians 2:10 declares that:

"We are His (God's) workmanship (creative handiwork) created unto good works!"

God does not specialize in making junk. The automobile manufacturers do that. The point is not the poor workmanship in your car, but the temporary, transitory nature of things. It is a law of nature that everything will eventually turn into junk. Mankind, on the other hand, was made in God's image and possesses His nature. Everyone is unique in design and purpose. God has no need for quality control. His works are always perfect, His ways are just. Make a choice to think: "I am God's special edition! I am unique! I was created for a special purpose, and I intend to fulfil it!"

7. REPENT FROM WORLDLY THOUGHT-PATTERNS

Bring your thought-life in line with your divine attachment. You have been grafted into God's Divine Nature. Since you now share Christ's resurrected life, live according to scriptural patterns.

8. REINFORCE YOUR POSITIVE MIND-SET

This is done by acting upon the information you have received. Start thinking, speaking and functioning in a productive and creative manner. Every time you do this, it will become easier to repeat the processes. Eventually it will become an habitual lifestyle.

"Search me, O God, and know my heart: try me, and know my thoughts." - Psalm 139:23

This is one key to successful living!

KEY 24   THINKING CAN BE A WASTE

Certain thought-processes can be a total waste of time. Indeed, some can be very destructive. Your thought-patterns must be controlled if happy and productive living is to be achieved. This is the import of Philippians 4:4-9:

> *"Rejoice in the Lord always: and again I say Rejoice. Let your moderation be known unto all men. The Lord is at hand. Be careful (anxious, full of care) for nothing; but in everything by prayer and supplication with thanksgiving let your requests be made known unto God. And the peace of God, which passeth all understanding, shall keep your hearts and minds through Christ Jesus. Finally, brethren, whatsoever things are honest, whatsoever things are just, whatsoever things are pure, whatsoever things are lovely, whatsoever things are of good report; if there be any praise,* **think on these things.** *Those things, which ye have both learned, and received, and heard, and seen in me,* **do***; and the God of peace shall be with you."*

Each one of us lives in two separate worlds at the same time. These worlds are as different from each other as night differs from day. Our dual citizenship gives us privileges and responsibilities in both worlds. Furthermore, we are accountable to the laws which govern each domain.

Living within the framework of these laws or principles guarantees a meaningful life. What are the two worlds in which I live? They are:

- the subjective inside world of feeling, and
- the objective outside world of reality.

1. THE WORLD OF INTERNAL SUBJECTIFICATIONS

The first world is internal. It is the private domain within. This is your kingdom. Here, you are sole Potentate, having full authority and exercising complete control. In this realm your imaginations and fantasies can reign freely. You can construct an empire just as you would like it to be. You are able to design each conquest and designate the outcome. It is a world where you can roam freely and without fear of interruption, interference or discovery. Since you are King, you are not accountable to anyone. No one else has any part in this world, except those whom you choose. It is a subjective world of feelings, thoughts, memories, hopes, fears, disappointments, preoccupations and regrets. It is a world of satisfying pleasures and noteworthy accomplishments. It may also take the form of painful defeat. Indeed, this world often becomes a hostile environment in which a person finds himself a fugitive, hiding in the sinister shadows of fear, failure, anxiety, jealousy, hate and bitterness.

2. THE WORLD OF EXTERNAL REALITIES

The second world is external. This is the outside world, the public domain without. It is the objective world of reality. It consists of other people, objects, things, events, responsibilities and a myriad of sensory perceptions such as sounds, smells and tastes. It is a world which is governed by time, space, politics, social order, money, health, and other people. It is governed by physical realities and is not affected by personal feelings. Here, the individual's role is just one small part of a massive whole. You are not monarch here. You are just one small part of a massive whole: Mr Average Citizen, who moves unnoticed through indifferent throngs.

An important exercise is to determine in which world you spend most of your time. Your answer to the following question is significant.

Question: Of all your wakeful cognitive hours, what percentage of your thinking time is spent in each world?

Answer: Subjective inside world of feeling
10% 40% 60% 90% More?

Objective outside world of reality
10% 40% 60% 90% More?

The majority of people spend more than ninety percent of their time in wasteful and destructive self-preoccupation. Like an ingrown toe nail, they have turned all their attention in on themselves. They rehearse each unpleasant event, thinking of novel ways in which they could have handled it differently. They carry the bitter feelings of each unjust thing which was said or done to them. They wrestle with painful memories, struggle with unpleasant emotions and contend with uncertainties. They seldom venture beyond the boarders of their subjective kingdom. The familiarity of the internal empire they have erected, offers a sense of morbid security. It is no wonder then, that life at its best becomes a tasteless existence.

Long before the word "psychology" was ever contrived, Isaiah (BC 712) pointed the way to relief:

"Thou wilt keep him in perfect peace, whose mind is stayed on thee because he trusteth in thee." - Isaiah 26:3

In modern psychological vernacular this verse would read something like this:

God will bring about emotional and mental stability to those whose thought-patterns are controlled by Him and who are anchored in His Word!

Thoughts must be productive and creative in nature. Before the automobile was invented, before high-rises were constructed, before aircraft took off, before computers were designed, they only existed as thoughts in someone's productive mind. If these people were preoccupied with their personal problems, we would still be living in pre-historic times. Let us think thoughts from God's perspective and not from man's view-point. Pattern your thought-life after eternal verities. Don't allow your mind to be cluttered with futile preoccupations.

"Search me, O God, and know my heart: try me, and know my thoughts: and see if there be any wicked way in me, and lead me in the way everlasting." - Psalm 139:23-24

"Examine me, O Lord, and prove me; try my reins and my heart." - Psalm 26:2

"Let this mind be in you, which was also in Christ Jesus." - Philippians 2:5

This is one key to successful living!

KEY 25   CAUSES FOR A NEGATIVE ATTITUDE

A positive attitude is vital to well-being. A healthy self-image, a confident outlook to the future and a happy disposition are imperative to successful living. In 1975 Reader's Digest carried an article written by a Harvard University research team. They discovered that the most important factor in motivation and job performance is the way a person habitually thinks about himself and his surroundings. Solomon (B C 1000) came to this same conclusion three thousand years earlier. He asserted that a man's well-being is directly proportionate to his thinking process. He gave us this maxim:

"For as a man thinketh in his heart, so is he." - *Proverbs 23:7*

Sadly, many people have accepted a very negative posture as the norm for their lives. This is made evident by the number of times we hear phrases such as:

- I'll never get it all done!
- Everything I eat goes to my hips!
- Every time I open my mouth, I get a shoe in it!
- With my luck, it will never happen!
- I guess I'm just a born loser!
- It's a wonder they put up with me!

- 20% chance of rain? What a lousy day!
- BAIK

One disoriented office worker carried a badge on his lapel which sported the letters BAIK. When asked what it meant, he would respond, "It means, Boy Am I Konfused!" "But that's spelled with a C!" would come the response. "That just goes to prove how Konfused I really am!" he would retort. He displayed his badge only in jest, but it was the dominant theme of his thinking. He was indeed "Konfused", and as a result, his work suffered. After several reprimands he was dismissed from the company. Here are some reasons for this type of destructive thinking:

1. FAULTY REARING

Whether deliberately or unknowingly, parents often plant the seeds of negativism in their children's minds. Positive approval is important to each child. This is evidenced by the frequency with which children strive for your attention. "Look Mommy! Watch me Daddy!" This thirst for attention is fertile ground for every seed, be it approval or rejection. Children are not the only people who need positive strokes. Adults need this kind of recognition as well. Wise and kind indeed is the person who can give it with sincerity.

2. NEGATIVE SOCIAL MIND-SET

I find our local meteorologists especially disheartening. The weatherman comes into my home every evening with his trusty weather map just as I am about to retire for the night. With "Konfusing" terms such as "Upslope", "Low Pressure" and "Frontal System" he warns me that a terrific storm is brooding in the deep Pacific and that in 5 days it could possibly dump much precipitation in the form of snow. My night's sleep is interrupted by nightmares of inundation. Visions of Arctic blizzards, snow, ice and its confining grips, preoccupy each wakeful moment. Unable to enjoy the spring-like sunshine, I wrestle with apprehension as I anticipate the depressive storm. Finally, the hour arrives and it thunders through with howling winds that pile snow in banks around the front door and cakes the corners of the window-sills.

Within two brief hours the storm is over and the sun is shining again, and I'm left to shovel away the unwarranted accumulation of fears and depression and frustration and such stuff.

Good news is seldom reported. The shocking, the unusual, the clandestine and the gory make the "scoop" and the bold headlines. "After all," we are told, "this is what's happening and it is news!" But somehow, all the contrary winds of values, events, philosophies and injustices tend to colour our moods and outlook on life. This is what prompted Isaiah (BC 712) to say:

"Thou (God) wilt keep him in perfect peace, whose mind is stayed on thee: because he trusteth in thee. Trust ye in the Lord for ever: for in the Lord **Jehovah** *is everlasting strength." - Isaiah 26:3-4*

Always be grateful that God is not influenced by the Weather Bureau, The Evening News or the Pole-taker's statistics. He is sovereign and His purposes will never be thwarted! It was Mark Twain who said: "There are lies, contemptible lies and statistics!"

3. NEGATIVE REINFORCEMENT

It has been said that money makes money, success breeds success, and the poor have children. The import of this is that both success and poverty tend to be self-reinforcing. One successful accomplishment encourages a second attempt. In a similar way, failures, reversals and disappointments tend to discourage any further motivation. "Why should I try? I would only fail again and I hate failure!" This was the sentiment expressed by a grade 10 drop-out. Such a person must be shown that he is not a failure at everything. He must be shown that he does have areas of strength. His successes must be reinforced with approval and recognition. Otherwise he is likely never to try anything.

4. HABITUAL THINKING

Thought-patterns are as habitual as actions. Automatically and without thought you get out of bed, dress and groom yourself, get in your car, start the engine and drive to work. You come out of your coma only when you enter your place of employment. Widely awake, you set yourself to your daily responsibilities. Most routine actions are done on auto-pilot. In a similar way, thinking runs the same pattern over and over again. An established mind-set is difficult to reprogram. However it can be done, and it must! Old mind patterns must be set aside. New ones must be established. The Apostle Paul underscores this need when he commands:

"Be not conformed to this world, but be ye transformed by the **renewing** *of your* **mind***." - Romans 12:2*

5. SAD-SACK FRIENDS

Your associations and relationships will influence your behaviour and thought-patterns. Peer pressure is the greatest influence leading to drug abuse and pregnancy among teenagers. A wise man once said, "Show me your friends, and I will tell you who you are!" We are influenced greatly by those around us. If you desire a different mind-set and life-style, it may be wise to choose some new friends.

Hang around Jesus, and note the change!

I once bought my daughter a budgie for a pet. The smiling sales person told me that if properly trained, the bird could speak seven languages. My daughter would place the cage near the window for the sunlight, while she was off at school. She spent hours training the budgie, but her faithful efforts produced only disappointment. All the bird could do was chirp like a sparrow. The reason became clear to us, only when it was too late. Outside her bedroom window was a large tree, a harbinger for neighbourhood sparrows! The influence which the sparrows exerted far outweighed my daughter's training efforts. Paul, the Apostle, addresses this subject clearly in his letter to the Roman Christians:

"Therefore, I urge you, brothers, in view of God's mercy, to offer your bodies as living sacrifices, holy and pleasing to God - which is your spiritual worship. Do not conform any longer to the pattern of this

world, but be transformed by the renewing of your mind. Then you will be able to test and approve what God's will is - his good, pleasing and perfect will." - Romans 12:1-2 (New International Version)

It is interesting to note that the word used for *conform* is *skemah* from which the English word *schematic* (blue prints, patterns, designs) is derived. Do no let the world be your *schematic* for behavioral patterns. The word *transformed* in the original Greek is *metamorphuse*. It is the derivative for the word, *metamorphosis*. It speaks of a change from the larva stage into adulthood.

This is one key for successful living!

KEY 26   SMILE AND KWITYERBELYAKIN!

Have you ever met a **Sad-Sack**? Do you happen to know one personally? The reference here is to a genuine, bona-fide sad- sack; the kind that finds pleasure only when things go wrong. Such people are seldom happy and frown a lot. They are critical of others and nothing good ever happens to them. As soon as the Sad-Sack swings his feet off the bed in the morning, and sets them on the cold floor, he knows it's going to be a bad day.

You will not find the word **kwityerbelyakin** in your dictionary or encyclopedia. An accurate definition, however, might read like this:

"A prohibition given to discourage verbal negativism; a strong vernacular warning against grumbling, muttering, whining, whimpering, snivelling and complaining."

During his lunch break, a factory worker drew a large happy face on his paper place mat. The smile extended from ear to ear. Beneath the huge smile he penned these words: **smile , and kwityerbelyakin!** The literal translation reads: "Smile and quit your belly aching!" It became a company slogan. The Personnel Manager saw the pencilled sketch and offered the artist $50.00 for his creativity. The cartoon later appeared in a nationwide promotional blitz, which garnered thousands of dollars in revenue. The Apostle Paul underscored the same thought in Philippians 4:4:

"Rejoice in the Lord always: and again I say rejoice!"

The Sad-Sack must know that the admonition does not read: "Belyake, and again I say belyake!" Happiness is the order of the day. Several important observations about happiness must be made. Peace and joy are not contingent upon circumstances. The source of happiness is found within. It is not discovered in the facts of life, but in the attitude of the heart. It needs no reason to function and it operates spontaneously. In referring to her friend's character, Rainer Maria Rilke wrote: "Her smile was not meant to be seen by anyone and served its whole purpose in being smiled!" There are times when it may be difficult to find happiness within yourself, but it is impossible to find it elsewhere!

Several years ago a newspaper offered a prize for the best definition of the word *money.* Hundreds of contestants submitted their definitions. The winning definition read as follows: *"money:* a universal provider of everything but happiness; and a passport to everywhere but to heaven."

Here are twenty important facts about a happy smile:
1. It costs nothing.
2. It is not beyond the financial reach of anyone.
3. It is easy to carry.
4. No special equipment is required to store it.
5. It never diminishes with use.
6. It has a lifetime guarantee.
7. It cannot be lost or stolen.
8. It cannot be misplaced or forgotten.
9. It can be activated instantaneously.
10. It requires no warm-up time to activate.
11. It multiplies itself spontaneously.
12. Its regenerating capabilities are phenomenal.
13. Its effect on others is long-lasting.
14. Its retention capabilities are enduring.
15. It brightens all shaded areas.

16. It lubricates relationships like oil.
17. It lightens burdens.
18. It is readily accepted by others.
19. It is understood in every culture.
20. It produces health, riches and well-being.

"If I could find an item that would do all that for me," said one wealthy heiress, "I'd pay big money for it!" The fact of the matter is that it could be hers and that it would cost her nothing. There is no one so poor and needy, so destitute and naked as he who has no smile to wear. Dress yourself up in your best attire; put on a smile! Determine to smile today. Life is too brief to spend it in the shadows of gloom and despair. Be happy!

The Old Testament prophet, Nehemiah, gives us a message of comfort in the midst of peril. The children of Israel had been in bondage in Babylon for seventy years. During the reign of Cyrus they were permitted to return to Jerusalem. When the small band of devotees returned, they found the city in ruins. The walls were broken down, the gates burned, the streets and road-ways overburdened with debris and the fields overgrown with decades of foliage. The task of rebuilding was overwhelming for so few. They had to contend with shortages, inconvenience, discouragement and militant opposition from neighbouring tribes. Despite numerous difficulties, the city was rebuilt under the leadership of Nehemiah.

His name is derived from two Hebrew words. The first word is *Nacham* meaning "to console or sigh with pity". The second word is *Yahh*, an abbreviation of God's name, Yah-Weh. The name Nehemiah means "The consolation of God!" You will find the books of Ezra and Nehemiah encouraging stories of purpose and courage in the midst of overwhelming odds and opposition. Hear his challenge:

"... *neither be ye sorry; for the joy of the* **Lord** *is your strength.*" - *Nehemiah 8:10*

This is one key to successful living!

KEY 27   HOW TO ACHIEVE MEDIOCRITY

Books with titles such as "How To Be A Low-Life", "Up A Dead-End Street" or "How To Achieve Mediocrity" will never top the best sellers list. Most people feel that their knowledge on the subject can equal that of any author. Furthermore, it is how to succeed that alludes and interests most people.

The word *mediocre* comes from two Latin and French words: *medi*, meaning half way, and *ocris* meaning mountain or mountain ledge. The literal translation means half way up the mountain! The mediocre person is satisfied with half measures. He is pleased with near accomplishments. Because the mediocre person is satisfied with marginal successes, he never discovers his full potential. He never sees life's glorious vistas from the top of the mountain, simply because he never scales its heights. He is satisfied to live *half way up the mountain*. It is highly improbable that the mediocre person will ever gain success. For those, however, who are interested in achieving mediocrity, for those who are satisfied with the ordinary commonplace status-quo, here are several good rules to follow. They will help you in becoming an amiable non-entity.

1. REJECT ALL CORRECTION OR INSTRUCTION

Reject every suggestion. Turn a deaf ear to every word of advice. Presume that all calls for change are but malicious criticism. This will effectively shield you from hostile intent. It is an effective defense against the harsh realities of failure, rejection and abuse. The serious danger, however, is that you will never learn anything about yourself or those around you. Solomon warned: *"The way of a fool seems right to him, but a wise man listens to advice."* - Proverbs 12:15 (New International Version)

2. ASSUME A SUPERIOR POSTURE

Presuppose that all tenderness, accommodation, congeniality and submission is a display of personal weakness. Such weakness is viewed as intolerable and must never be acknowledged. This stance will ensure your credibility as one of strength, courage and self-sufficiency. The danger here is that it leads to exaggerated independence. The hog which finds itself stranded in the centre of the frozen barn yard pond, resists every attempt of help, yet it is totally helpless to help itself. Humans are social beings, and therefore need each other. The byproducts of a humble attitude are many, and they include such dynamics as positive approval, encouragement, social interchange, interpersonal transaction and personal help.

3. LIE A LOT - ESPECIALLY TO YOURSELF

Never acknowledge a need for improvement; never say "I'm sorry!"; never admit that you have "blown it!" and above all, never concede that you are wrong. Theorize that those who do are little more than wimps. Alleviate your guilt and uneasiness by telling yourself that you were justified in your actions. You must rationalize that your behaviour was appropriate for the occasion and then project the blame for your reactions onto others. The peril here is self-deception.

Jeremiah (BC 601) declared that man's " *heart is deceitful above all things, and desperately wicked.*" - Jeremiah 17:9

The tendency of the human heart is to form reality as we would like it to be, despite fact. The paradise we live in may be but a vain delusion, and since we concede to no wrong, there can be no deliverance.

4. ENJOY EXPEDIENCY - IF IT FEELS GOOD, DO IT

Do it. Whatever is good for the now, do it! Regardless of the consequences, do it. Do what? Whatever you wish: sleep in the extra hour, go in late for work, eat that extra piece of pie, blow off at the mouth, tell your superiors off, drive a hundred miles (160 km) per hour, express vulgarity and anything your impulses may urge. Surmise that unrestrained and uninhibited venting of personal urges is **in the now** and belongs to those of the "Pepsi generation". Those who believe in self-control belong to the "Geritol geriatrics!" However, self-denial is a main ingredient for growth and development. They who resist self-denial, place themselves in jeopardy of insignificance. Jesus instructed His disciples with these words:

"If any man will come after me, let him deny himself, and take up his cross, and follow me. For whosoever will save his life shall lose it: and whosoever will lose his life for my sake shall find it." - *Matthew 16:24-25*

5. LIST TWENTY REASONS WHY YOU CAN'T

Speculate that it is the objective, intelligent and discerning mind that can quickly see all the iniquities. After all, is it not the wise man who counts the cost before building any tower? Yes indeed! But the wise man sees the potential also. The hazard here is that the negative mind-set will project negative attitudes into everything he sees. To the jaundiced eye, the whole world looks yellow. He who can quickly list 20 good reasons why he can't, will find difficulty in finding any reasons why he can.

6. AVOID ALL RISKS AT ANY COST

Believe that the prudent man never gambles on the future. A bird in hand is worth two in the bush. A stable person operates in the realm of certainties only. This attitude affords a great deal of comfort, if comfort is uppermost in your thinking. But it pre-empts the pioneering spirit. No pioneering venture is without its discomforts, uncertainties and risks. If Columbus had this mind-set we would all be living in Europe. If Edison had this philosophy we would all be watching television in the dark. Without risk, the West would never have been settled. If Orvil and Wilbur had obeyed their father, the Reverend Bishop Wright, we would still be walking. "If God had intended us to fly, He would have made us with wings!" chided their father. But they persisted in their "inane foolishness", risking their lives, until that memorable day in 1903 at Kitty Hawk where the first air flight was shorter than the wing-span of a 747. The rest is history.

7. IF AT FIRST YOU DON'T SUCCEED, NUTS TO IT

It is thought that effectiveness is the measure of success in relationship to the effort expended. If too much energy is used in achieving a certain goal, change your goal. The danger here is that some great achievement may never be accomplished, simply because we stopped too soon. It is not a well-known fact, yet true, that Thomas Edison had over 1 000 experimental failures before inventing the incandescent lamp. All we see today is the light. We seldom stop to realize that Babe Ruth had 1330 strike-outs in baseball. All we remember him for is his home run record. Keep swinging!

Mediocrity is a blight to mankind. We are made in the image of God. His very nature is creative. Status-quo was never God's intent for His children. He delights in your productivity. Invest your talents to serve Him and to influence those around you positively. However, if mediocrity is your goal, you will find these seven simple steps helpful in achieving it!

This is one key to successful living!

KEY 28   THE QUAGMIRE OF PUBLIC OPINION

Public opinion has been elevated to a position where it is used as a "golden rule" to measure normality. The word *normal* can be defined as, *an established standard, rule, or principle; the average or mean value of desirable qualities.* What the majority of any group, sampling or society deems best, is considered the norm. Hence it is concluded that any disagreement with the majority, or the norm, is a "deviation."

1. FACTS ABOUT POPULAR OPINION

The news media places great importance on public opinion polls. These are conducted on a variety of subjects ranging from presidential election debates to the belief in UFO's. The results are interpreted as "normal thinking". The polls, however, only serve as reinforcements to perpetuate themselves and legitimise the poll-takers salary. Projections based on statistics can be very misleading. It was Mark Twain who said, "There are lies, contemptible lies and then there are statistics!" in that order of severity. Here are some things you should remember when placing your trust in public opinion polls.

1.1 Statistics can be deliberately misleading

The results of public opinion polls can be deliberately skewed by the very questions which are asked. For example, the question may be asked:

"Do you believe in war?" The obvious answer is "no". The results of that poll could be reported in this manner: On the subject of nuclear weaponry or military funding, 1 000 people were asked if they believed in war. Virtually 100% of those polled said no. The conclusion presented is obvious: The average thinking man, and by far the majority, believe in disarmament.

1.2 Statistic can be purposely biased

The results of a public opinion poll can be biased by the sampling taken. For example, the question may be asked, "Do you prefer living in a city or in the country?" The results will vary depending upon whether the poll was taken in large cities like London, Houston, Toronto, Johannesburg or in rural agrarian areas such as Kansas, Saskatchewan or the Karoo.

1. 3 Statistics can be intentionally partial

The results of the poll can be misleading in that the part polled is assumed to be representative of the whole, plus or minus three percentage points. For example, I may want to determine whether or not there is more poverty in our city than there was twenty years ago. Suppose the poll-taker went downtown and interviewed 1 000 people from the Rescue Mission, Salvation Army, Volunteers of America, and the ghetto. What do you suppose their answer would be? A poll conducted in a suburban area would be markedly different.

1.4 Statistics cannot exclude the "Fickle Factor"

Public opinion is as changeable as the weather. The Harris and the Gallop polls have proven that. Matthew 21:8-9 records Jesus Christ's triumphant entry into Jerusalem as King of Kings on Palm Sunday. The multitudes shouted: "*Hosanna to the highest.*" They shaded him with palm leaves and paved his path with their cloaks. Several days later, the same crowd hissed at him, spat in His face, and cried, "*Crucify him, and let his blood be upon us and our children.*"

2. SAD RESULTS CAUSED BY POPULAR OPINION

How exacting is the science of public opinion? Does that question need an answer? Yes, indeed! Public opinion is made to represent a trend or a norm, and the degree of divergence from that standard is called **deviation**. People who protected the Jews during World War II were called abnormal. A person who wears a three-piece suit to the beach is seen as inappropriately dressed. All cannibals consider those who refuse to eat human flesh as peculiar. To them, a steak of human rump served on a platter is quite normal, but this is not the best way to serve mankind! Despite its distorted representation of reality, public opinion is such a strong force that many are powerless to resist it. Those who succumb to the pressures of public opinion can expect some regrettable results, such as:

2.1 Succumbing to the influence of peer pressure

Because of peer pressure, teenagers will abandon their own convictions. Peer pressure is the most important factor leading to drug abuse and teenage pregnancies. Mob violence is senseless and brutal. Those who have been swept away in the heat of this emotion will acknowledge that they were moved against their better judgment. Stand up for your convictions.

2.2 Feelings of inferiority and inadequacy

Respect for public opinion is most confining. Fear of rejection is the main ingredient of the inferiority complex. For this reason many will inhibit self-expression. These are the fearful who prefer to do nothing, lest what is done is not acceptable to the majority. Franklin P Jones had a healthy philosophy of public opinion when he said: "Wearing shorts usually reveals nothing more about a man than his indifference to public opinion!" Be proud of your individuality and your uniqueness.

2.3 Obstructed growth and progress

Status-quo offers a measure of security. Adventure moves you beyond your comfort zone, and exposes you to the risk of failure and rejection.Those who are afraid to venture outside their comfort-zone, must contend with stagnation. The fear of failure and the demeaning consequences of public rejection will pre-empt all venture or invention. Go ahead and try!

2.4 Frustrated personal motivation and incentive

Many people will abdicate their rights. Controversial issues such as abortion, sexual perversion, humanism and hedonism are never addressed. The consequence is that controversial behaviour spreads like a contagious disease without check. "Most people are other people," said Oscar Wilde. "Their thoughts are someone else's opinions, their life a mimicry, their passions a quotation!" Be yourself.

3. DEFICIENCIES CREATED BY POPULAR OPINION

There are other dynamics, resulting from majority consensus, which are even more frightening. Many people find themselves bogged down in the quagmire of public opinion. For the Christian this can be a serious detriment.

3.1 Personal witness is pre-empted

Because they fear the opinion of peers and associates, many believers become closet Christians. Their witness to the faith has become non-existent. They have become as salt which has lost its savour. Be bold, be strong, for the Lord your God is with you!

3.2 Praise and worship is inhibited

Every Christian has a desire to develop an intimate relationship with Jesus. This longing never comes to fruition because of timidity. "I'm afraid my church friends will think I'm a fanatic or a holy roller," said one struggling saint. It must be remembered that, by definition, a fanatic is someone who loves Jesus more than I do! In a similar way, an heretic is someone who is not as spiritual as I am. Free expression has always been criticised by those who are bound. "Loyalty to a petrified opinion has never yet broken a chain or freed a human soul!" said Mark Twain.

3.3 Christian influence is negated

The organized church at large has become impotent. The following example illustrates this point. The mayoral candidates for a large USA city gave the homosexuals an audience in their mayoral election. They gave no audience to Christians! Do you know why? Because Christian churches were so divided against each other that no collective body could be organized. We are too busy proving that our doctrine is the only way. We guard our own little turf with such jealousy, that the rest of the world can go to hell without objection. The scriptures declare: *"Where the righteous reign there is rejoicing in the streets."* The Bible states that *"Righteousness exalts a nation."* May God grant unto us missionaries who will lead us in London, Ottawa, Washington, Pretoria and every seat of government. Let's call them politicians. May the Lord send missionaries to the darkest head-hunting tribe in the world, our education system. Here, dehumanizing humanism is promoted, whilst the slaughter of millions of children, through abortion, is promulgated. Let us call these missionaries teachers. If every Christian would recognize that his profession or vocation is essentially a ministry, and be bold in his witness, our influence would be impacting!

3.4 Christian outreach is hampered

Many people are denied an answer to their problems. The only example of Christ they may ever see, happens to be walking in your shoes. If you are hesitant in your witness to the truth, others may never see it. How tragic! Suppose for one moment that your neighbour's house was on fire. What would you do? Would you hesitate to call him lest he be angry because you disturbed him? You would never question whether it was convenient or not. You would urgently warn him. I assure you he would thank you.

3.5 The salt has lost its savour

Society, in general, views the church as irrelevant. They see Christianity as a non-essential harbinger of archaic superstitions and relics. Why is this concept so prevalent? Because the world around us never hears us talking about Jesus, seldom sees us attending God's house and rarely sees us expressing our spiritual convictions. After all, we don't want public opinion to think despairingly of our professionalism ... now do we?

Does this sound like a guilt trip to you? It is not intended to be one. This is a challenge to extricate Christians from the quicksand of peer pressure and public opinion. Have the courage to identify yourself and live according to your convictions. If you don't have any, it is time to develop some. If you don't stand for something, you will likely fall for anything. Proverbs 29:25 asserts that:

"Fear of man will prove to be a snare, but whoever trusts in the Lord is kept safe."

Joshua 1:9 states:

"Have I not commanded you? Be strong and courageous. Do not be terrified; do not be discouraged, for the Lord your God will be with you wherever you go." (New International Version)

This is one key to successful living!

KEY 29   HOW TO DEVELOP CHARACTER

There is a vast difference between **attention** and **recognition** . The World Book Dictionary defines the word *recognition* as: "favourable notice; acknowledgment conveying approval or sanction." Positive acknowledgment is usually earned and is given as a reward to those showing character or accomplishment. Attention can be gained by loud noise, unusual dress or behaviour, inappropriate actions, reckless indifference or abrasive assertiveness. Any deviation from accepted norms will bring attention.

The desire for recognition is normal. Because we are social creatures, satisfaction is gained from the interchange and approval of others. The desire to be known and accepted by our peers is both natural and healthy. When the cost of earning recognition is seen as too great, some will settle for attention. The latter is never satisfying. Neither is it beneficial.

The world community is searching for men and women of character. When they are found, they are recognized and accepted as leaders. Who are these people? Let me suggest a thought-provoking exercise. Listed below are twenty identifying attributes of a person of character. Read each characteristic slowly. Determine whether it describes you. Ask yourself whether this is one of your qualities? Answer the question by placing a check mark in the appropriate column as: No___, Some times___, Usually___, Most often___, Yes___

Is this one of your qualities?

People of character are they who:

1. Place their character and integrity above wealth or position. They will not sell their credibility for personal gain or as a "get rich quick scheme". They will not jeopardize their reputation. Is this true of you?

No ___ Some times ___ Usually ___ Most often ___ Yes ___

2. Are directed by a well-built philosophy and a proven value system, rather than by public opinion. They are not influenced by the herd instinct which motivates most people. Is this true of you?

No ___ Some times ___ Usually ___ Most often ___ Yes ___

3. Whose word is as certain as a legal document. Their word is their honour and surety. A change in circumstance does not result in a change of commitment. Their yes is yes, and their no is no. Is this true of you?

No ___ Some times ___ Usually ___ Most often ___ Yes ___

4. Maintain their individuality in a group. They will not compromise their standards to gain corporate approval or advantage. Is this true of you?

No ___ Some times ___ Usually ___ Most often ___ Yes ___

5. Stand by their convictions against a rising tide of popular opinion. They are able to say no to questionable activities. They are willing to voice their opposition to error, even though it may be unpopular to do so. Is this true of you?

No ___ Some times ___ Usually ___ Most often ___ Yes ___

6. Are not motivated by selfish ambition or greed. They will not be bribed. Personal advantage is secondary to law and order. Is this true of you?

No ___ Some times ___ Usually ___ Most often ___ Yes ___

7. Will go the extra mile on behalf of another. They will inconvenience themselves for another's benefit, expecting nothing in return. They can be counted upon for help in a time of need. Is this true of you?

No ___ Some times ___ Usually ___ Most often ___ Yes ___

8. Do not mistake brazen bravado for courage or strength. They seek no attention nor take occasion for personal promotion. They are more interested in getting a job done, than who will gain the glory. Is this true of you?

No ___ Some times ___ Usually ___ Most often ___ Yes ___

9. Will defend truth at the expense of personal advantage. Like the Patriarch of old, they will keep their word, even to their own hurt. They can be depended upon for accurate witness. Is this true of you?

No ___ Some times ___ Usually ___ Most often ___ Yes ___

10. Are able to say **yes** and **no** with conviction. They do not vacillate between two opinions. Their word today can be depended upon tomorrow. Their speech carries credibility and authenticity. Is this true of you?

No ___ Some times ___ Usually ___ Most often ___ Yes ___

11. Have carry-through when no progress is apparent. Projects started are carried through to its completion. Like the Olympic runner who finished his marathon 18 hours late, they can respond, "My country sent me to finish the race, not just to start it!" Is this true of you?

No ___ Some times ___ Usually ___ Most often ___ Yes ___

12. Are responsible and faithful when appreciation and recognition are lacking. They can hand out the crisp new church bulletins during Sunday Worship, but also pick up old mutilated ones from the church floor Monday morning. Is this true of you?

No ___ Some times ___ Usually ___ Most often ___ Yes ___

13. Will be faithful to a friend through good times and bad. They will not abandon a friend who is in need. They will not avoid him when he is disgraced. They are not ashamed to associate with those who are less honourable. Is this true of you?

No ___ Some times ___ Usually ___ Most often ___ Yes ___

14. Will be quick to see another's good points, while slow to recognize the weak. They do not carry a judgmental attitude. They are able to complement another's strengths and overlook the flaws. Is this true of you?

No ___ Some times ___ Usually ___ Most often ___ Yes ___

15. Can disagree amicably. They are able to allow others to have and express their opinion. They can make allowances and display tolerances for another way of doing things. They do not have to have their way. Is this true of you?

No ___ Some times ___ Usually ___ Most often ___ Yes ___

16. Can accept another's individuality. They recognize the value and worth of others, and seek opportunity to benefit from diversity. They possess a teachable spirit. Is this true of you?

No ___ Some times ___ Usually ___ Most often ___ Yes ___

17. Display resiliency in the face of reversals. They do not give in to reversals or defeat. They bounce back under trial. They view each set-back as a stepping-stone to further victory. Is this true of you?

No ___ Some times ___ Usually ___ Most often ___ Yes ___

18. Show adaptability in unpleasant circumstances. They are able to adapt to unpleasantness as well as to unexpected favour. Is this true of you?

No ___ Some times ___ Usually ___ Most often ___ Yes ___

19. Are not motivated by personal comforts. They are not oriented by hedonistic self-gratification and do not see effort, hard work or discipline as an inconvenience. Is this true of you?

No ___ Some times ___ Usually ___ Most often ___ Yes ___

20. View life with hope and optimism. These people see the dark cloud but they are also able to see its silver lining. They entertain no pessimism and have no time for negativism. Is this true of you?

No ___ Some times ___ Usually ___ Most often ___ Yes ___

"Out of suffering," wrote E H Chapin, "have emerged the strongest souls; the most massive characters are seared with scars!" President Richard M Nickson stated, "We are faced with a choice between the work ethic that built this nation's character and the new welfare ethic that could cause the American character to weaken!" Solomon summarizes this succinctly in Proverbs 22:1:

"A good name is rather to be chosen than great riches, and loving favour rather than silver and gold."

This is one key to successful living!

KEY 30   SIMPLE FORMULAS FOR SUCCESS

The world around us is governed by established principles. Many of these laws can be reduced to simple formulas. We learn some of these formulas in high school. For example: the angles at the base of an isosceles triangle are equal; the opposite angles of two intersecting straight lines are equal; water is formulated from hydrogen and oxygen; for every action there is a reaction; etc. Such formulas have been determined by repeated observation and analysis. Because the dynamics are constant, the results can be predicted with absolute accuracy.

The renowned German rocket scientist, Dr Weorner Van Braun, contributed much to the American space program. I vividly recall a lecture that he gave in Lexington, Kentucky, on the exploration of space. The space shuttle was just a blue-print on the drawing board. Propulsion was a great obstacle. The following are excerpts of his discourse, taken from the notes which were made that evening:

"... We need two different types of engines in this space vehicle. The first is a rocket engine to project us into orbit, and push us around space; and the second, an air-breathing engine to propel us in earth's atmosphere on our return home. If we do that, however, the weight of the vehicle will be so heavy that we won't be able to carry a pay-load! To solve this problem, we do away with one of the engines.

We need the rocket engine to get into space, so the only one left to omit is the air-breathing engine. When we fall out of earth's orbit back to earth, we will have no power whatever. It will be like flying a gigantic kite! We will glide back home. That means that we have only one opportunity to make it back safely! But that should not be a problem. We know the weight of the spacecraft. We know the laws of gravity. We know the principles of aerodynamics. We know the laws which govern motion. We are well aware of the location and length of the runway, and much more. **If we obey these laws, and operate with their limitations, we can guarantee success!** We can determine the exact place and time and speed at which the space shuttle will land! We will have success!"

His words rang with the clarity of a bell! It suddenly became clear to me that knowing the laws which govern such dynamics as health, relationships, attitudes and well-being, and learning to function within their limitations, can guarantee successful living with absolute certainty! The contrary is also true. Any violation of these principles will produce ill effects. It is a sobering thought that the burden of responsibility for success or failure rests on the individual's doorstep. This is what Jesus taught in his parable in Matthew 7:24-27:

"Therefore whosoever heareth these sayings of mine, and doeth them, I will liken him unto a wise man, which built his house upon a rock: And the rain descended, and the floods came, and the winds blew, and beat upon that house; and it fell not: for it was founded upon a rock. And every one that heareth these words of mine, and doeth them not, shall be likened unto a foolish man, which built his house upon the sand: And the rain descended, and the floods came, and the winds blew, and beat upon that house; and it fell: and great was the fall of it."

If we obey established laws, we can guarantee success.

Here are seven simple formulas that you should know. Living your life within their limitations, will ensure a successful and purposeful life:

1. FORMULA 1: D + (M-D) = A

Determination increases **motivation**, decreases **discouragement** and results in **achievement**. Henry Ford determined to manufacture a horseless carriage so inexpensively that everyone could afford one. His achievement is known as the Ford Motor Company. Today we can ride in comfort!

2. FORMULA 2: GS + (P-S) = A

Goal setting increases **purpose**, decreases **stagnation** and results in **attainment**. Thomas Edison's goal was to bring light to a dimly-lit world. His purpose was to find an alternative light- source for fire. Although he had more than one thousand failures while experimenting, he continued his research. No one needs to sit in the dark! We have all benefitted from his attainment. It is a certainty that if you do not have a goal and do not know where you are going, you will not know how to get there. Set your goals, then go!

3. FORMULA 3: F + (H-W) = R

Faith increases **hope**, decreases **worry** and results in **reward**. The New Land Voyages of the May Flower lost two-thirds of their passengers within the first year. They were overcome by isolation, uncertainty, hunger and disease, but our Pilgrim Fathers had faith in God. Their hope made them our Founding Fathers as they gave birth to a new nation, the United States of America. Hope thou in God!

4. FORMULA 4: C + (D-A) = A

Commitment increases **direction**, decreases **ambivalence** and results in **accomplishment**. Babe Ruth struck out 1 330 times, more than any other baseball player before him, but he never allowed his bad press to discourage him. His commitment to the game earned him the title of Home-Run King, a record which he held for almost two decades. Keep swinging!

5. FORMULA 5: P + (O-U) = P

Planning increases **organization**, decreases **uncertainty** and results in **productivity**. Random selection can never produce order. This is one obvious fact that the evolutionists ignore. An explosion in a publishing house will never produce a dictionary. The man who dynamites his Volkswagen in the hope that the pieces will randomly fall together as a Mercedes, will be sadly disappointed. The only consequence of random choosing is disorder and confusion. Life is a matter of choice! Making the right choices affect every facet of life. Joshua offers his people a choice which would greatly affect their destiny. He charged them with these words: *"Choose you this day whom ye will serve."* He later declared his intentions with these words, *"As for me and my house, we will serve the Lord."* - Joshua 24:15

6. FORMULA 6: E + (P-A) = S

Endurance increases **patience**, decreases **agitation** and results in **stability**. Nothing can be added to improve Paul's discourse on this subject. His testimony comes from years of experience. It will do us well to receive his encouragement.

"... but we glory in tribulations also: knowing that tribulation worketh patience; And patience, experience; and experience, hope: And hope maketh not ashamed ..." - Romans 5:3-5

"... let us lay aside every weight, and the sin which doth so easily beset us, and let us run with patience the race that is set before us, Looking unto Jesus ... For consider him that endured such contradiction of sinners against himself, lest ye be wearied and faint in your minds. Ye have not yet resisted unto blood, striving against sin ... Wherefore lift up the hands which hang down, and the feeble knees; And make straight paths for your feet ... Follow peace ... Looking diligently, lest any man fail of the grace of God; lest any root of bitterness springing up trouble you, and thereby many be defiled." -   Hebrews 12: 1-4, 12-15

7. FORMULA 7: E + (E-N) = S

Expectation increases **enthusiasm**, decreases **negativism** and results in **success**. Expectation is self-fulfilling. Whether you believe in failure or success, you will be rewarded accordingly. Historical Job lamented:

"The thing which I greatly feared, is come upon me." - Job 3:25.

Your expectation of health and prosperity is God's desire for you. This is clearly demonstrated by the salutation of John:

"Beloved, I wish above all things that thou mayest prosper and be in health, even as thy soul (mental expectation or mind-set) prospereth."
- 3 John 2

These formulas will work. They have been tried in the crucible of time and have been found dependable.

This is one key to successful living!

KEY 31   SICK STANDARDS FOR SELF-IMAGE

Everyone has the need to feel good about himself. The need for recognition and acceptance is universal. When this is not forthcoming, self-image is greatly affected. Those who question their ability or worth, constantly struggle with fears about their performance. If a person feels that he has nothing to say, it is a certainty that he will avoid proving it. "After all," he thinks, "I would rather have people think that I am a dummy, than open my mouth and dissolve any doubt they may have had!" Those who fear failure are unlikely to attempt anything involving risk. Failure would only confirm their assessment and reinforce their negative self-image. Rather than running that risk, they attempt nothing. Please underscore this fact in your thinking: **Self-worth must never be determined by external standards!**

We usually judge our worth by comparing ourselves to other people and the standards and values they have established. If we measure up to these standards, we approve of ourselves and feel worthy of the approval of others. How well we perform among our peers, becomes the basis upon which we determine our self-worth. This entire process is defective! Here are four reasons why self-worth must never be determined by external standards:

1. PERFORMANCE DOES NOT DETERMINE VALUE

Your value is not determined by how well you perform, but rather by who you are. Parents, teachers, employers and the church often link value and performance. This is evidenced by the frequency with which we hear such admonitions as: "Johnny, please carry out the trash like a good boy! Jenny, make your bed like a good girl! Bring home an "A" on your report card like a good student!" This teaches me that my self-worth is directly proportionate to my performance. Those who have been programmed with such a mind-set will struggle in adulthood. The large income becomes proof that a businessman is successful; the accumulation of things ensures a person's importance; and faithful attendance every time the church doors are open is certain proof that you are a good Christian! The end result is a relentless drive to prove self-worth.

By nature, life itself is a series of struggles, trials and errors. If failure has been made the measuring rod of self-worth, then failure should be avoided at all cost. Failure, however, is an undeniable reality of life. We frequently fail as parents, mates, friends and neighbours. As a model Christian, I often fall far short of my own standards. When such failure does occur, it produces guilt, self-condemnation and feelings of worthlessness.

The fact that you have failed, does not prove that you are a failure. That line of reasoning would logically lead a person to conclude that he is a horse, simply because he visited a barn. The truth of the matter is that failure only proves that you have been trying. The only way children can learn to ride a bicycle, is to pick themselves up every time they fall down! This is true for every discipline in life. Learning how to master failure, is the only way to succeed.

2. CONFORMITY DOES NOT ESTABLISH VALUE

The desire for acceptance and recognition is the primary reason for conformity to peer pressure. Self-image should not be determined by external social values. These standards are variable and inexact. There are always shifting opinions and differing ideals and goals which are beyond reach. Since all these standards cannot be accommodated at one time, the constant struggle to appease them can only create a failure syndrome. This in turn causes feelings of inferiority, inadequacy, guilt and failure.

High school and college students are particularly affected by peer pressure. So great is their desire for acceptance by the *In Crowd* that many will compromise their morals and convictions. To their regret, they later discover that the price they paid was far too great, and the acceptance they gained was only an empty delusion. Never be afraid to live by your own convictions! Be a trend-setter by positively influencing those around you. You will discover that it will only increase your sense of self-worth.

3. STATUS DOES NOT AUTHENTICATE PERSONAL VALUE

Such things as position, rank, class, possessions or station in life, cannot validate self-worth. We must not judge our value by comparing ourselves to others. The opinion of others whom we admire and trust can be helpful in providing insights, but cannot be the criteria by which we examine ourselves. The opinions of other people are as varied as their faces. The Bible is the only standard which does not fluctuate with the passage of time. Politics, possessions or popular opinion can never deny or confirm merit. Peter provides a standard which should enhance every Christian's self-image. His statement is authoritative and can be trusted:

> *"Once you were less than nothing; now you are God's own. Once you knew very little of God's kindness; now your very lives have been changed by it."* - 1 Peter 2:10 (The Living Bible)

4. GOD'S WORD ALONE VERIFIES PERSONAL VALUE

Each one of us has been made in the image of God. Whether you fail or succeed does not alter that fact! You carry in your being the nature of Him who created you. The very nature of God is to be creative, productive, loving and confident. Since this is true, you are capable of displaying the same characteristics. You must accept yourself as you are. Never be ashamed to be you or afraid to attempt anything. Failure or success is not an issue. Let God succeed through you! This was Paul's encouragement to the Christian's at Corinth:

"I thank my God always on your behalf, for the grace of God which is given you by Jesus Christ; That in every thing ye are enriched by him, in all utterance, and in all knowledge; Even as the testimony of Christ was confirmed in you: So that you come behind in no gift; waiting for the coming of our Lord Jesus Christ: who shall also confirm you unto the end, that ye may be blameless in the day of our Lord Jesus Christ."
- 1 Corinthians 1:4-8

Performance is the consequence of self-worth!

Performance, then, is the consequence of self-worth and not the proof. Never is self-worth to be determined by performance. There is no reason for anyone to have a poor, paralysing self-image. Accept yourself for who you are. Recognize that God created you as he desired you to be. Wherein you have deviated, He has provided correction, instruction and strength to change. Your worth has been established by the enormous price Jesus paid for your salvation at Calvary. Because of God's grace, you can feel worthy. Let God perform the creating of His image in you!

"For all who are led by the Spirit of God are the sons of God. And so we should not be like cringing, fearful slaves, but we should behave like God's very own children ... For His Holy Spirit speaks to us deep in our hearts, and tells us that we are really God's Children. And since we are his children, we will share his treasure - for all God gives to his Son Jesus is now ours too!" - Romans 8:14-17 (The Living Bible)

This is one key to successful living!

KEY 32   A BUTTERFLY OR A WORM?

Two caterpillars were crawling along the ground, painfully pushing their way through debris in search of fodder. Looking up, they saw the majestic monarch butterfly, fluttering effortlessly above them. The one looked at the other and said: "Boy, you'll never get me up in one of those things!" But, the caterpillar is merely the larva stage of the adult butterfly. At full maturity, each caterpillar will fly in "one of those things". This requires a process known as metamorphosis. Webster defines metamorphosis as:

"a change in physical form, structure or substance, esp. by supernatural means."

The Apostle Paul used this example in his plea for a personality change:

"*... And be not conformed to this world, but be ye transformed by the renewing of your mind.*" *- Romans 12:2*

A personality change is more than a possibility or a plausibility, it is a command: "*Be ye transformed!*" The word which is used for *transformed,* means *metamorphosis.* Be ye *transformed,* that is, undergo a metamorphic change. This challenge is for all the "brethren". If you are tired of your mind-set, life style and emotional demeanour, then this charge is for you. There is hope for those who determine, "I have lived in this sub-standard state long enough! I refuse to be subjected to this ground level litter any longer! There is more in life for me than what I am experiencing. I will submit myself to that changing process and fly to new heights!" If this is your resolve, you could very well be entering one of the most exciting and revolutionary periods of your life.

This metamorphic process can be likened to the tugging, pushing, stretching and pulling actions of the butterfly as it escapes the confines of the chrysalis. It begins with a total disgust for the limitations we find ourselves in. Then follows the keen desire for something different, something more than what we have learned to accept as norm. Like a morning sunrise, it gradually dawns on us that we were created for better and higher things. Then follows a determination to **turn away from** the former confines, and a **turning unto** a new freedom. Actually, this is an excellent illustration of the word "repentance".

It is interesting to note that this metamorphic or transforming process is a mind function: *"Be ye transformed by the renewing of your mind."* It is an accepted fact that all human behaviour is predicted upon a mind-set. Solomon confirmed this fact when he declared, *"As a man thinketh, so is he."* When a man's mind is conditioned to think along certain avenues, his feet will carry him to the shops that are located there. Thinking negatively activates negative behaviour. Think garbage, act garbage! Think depression, and you will crawl like some worm through the circumstantial debris of unhappy memories, ambivalent emotions and broken dreams.

The particular mind function which brings about change is called "Renewing". There are many synonyms for the word *renew*: re- establish, rejuvenate, recreate, rebuild and refresh are but a few. The word *renew*, means to change in form or substance. The entire process of change begins with such a mind renewal. It does not end in mental gymnastics, however. It affects every facet of life. We literally become new persons, having new goals, new interests and new desires. It is an experience that offers new direction, attitude and motivation. It is like being "born again" as a different person into a different world.

Webster said that metamorphosis was a "change ... esp. by a supernatural means". Indeed, it is supernatural! Instead of allowing the world's concepts to fill your mind, let God's concepts renew you. His precepts are contained in a book called the Bible, and they were demonstrated to us in the life of One called Jesus. His single purpose for coming to earth was to bring about this change. Available to everyone who receives Him, is this "newness of life".

Make every effort to bring your thinking process under the direct control of God's Spirit. Command your mind to fall in line with the directives of God's Word. Let God's divine affirmations occupy your mind. In everyday modern vernacular, here is what you can confidently declare:

I am a winner! - 2 Corinthians 2:14

I am an adequate person! - 2 Corinthians 9:8

I am unique and special! - 1 Peter 2:9

My life has meaning and purpose! - Ephesians 2:10

As a person, I am successful! - Psalm 1:1-3

I am strong and able! - Psalm 27:1

I am sufficient for every task! - 2 Peter 1:8-10

I will overcome every obstacle! - John 16:33

Reversals will not subdue me! - 1 John 4:4

Designs to harm me shall fail! - Isaiah 54:17

I am secure and confident! - Proverbs 3:24-26

Under trial, I will stand! - 1 Corinthians 10:13

My works shall prosper! - 1 Kings 2:2-3

I am well supplied! - Psalm 34:9-10

Health and prosperity are mine! - 3 John 2

My needs are always met! - Philippians 4:19

I have everything I need! - 2 Peter 1:3-4

I am well and healthy! - Matthew 8:16-17

My thoughts are affirmative! - Philippians 4:4-9

My worries are over! - 1 Peter 5:7

Fear is not my practice! - 2 Timothy 1:7

I am a totally new person! - 2 Corinthians 5:17

I am living abundantly! - John 10:10

I am happy, happy, happy! - Philippians 4:4

I am free, I'm free! - John 8:32, 36

All this is true, and I believe it! - Numbers 23:19

These laws are written in my mind! - Hebrews 8:10

I envision each affirmation! - 1 Chronicles 29:18

God is my (YHWH), my I Am! - Exodus 3:14

I am complete in Christ Jesus! - Colossians 2:10

Because of Jesus Christ I am and I can! - Philippians 4:13

Read each divine affirmation daily. Do this out loud, so that your ears can hear your mouth. Read them with conviction. Memorize one scripture each week, until all can be recited by memory. Meditate on one scripture each day. Envision the affirmation you are memorizing. Follow these instructions as your passport to successful living.

"Lord Jesus, I'm tired of crawling through life like a caterpillar. There is more in life for me than this painful existence. I desire this new kind of life. Come into my life with Your presence and precepts. Make me a new person. Help me to fly, where now I can only crawl. I pray this in and through the name of your Son, Jesus Christ. Amen."

This is one key to successful living!

KEY 33   PRIDE IS TOO EXPENSIVE

You can't afford it! Pride is too expensive a commodity to own. There is a vast difference between **pride** and **self-esteem**. Self- esteem is a feeling of personal acceptance and worth. It can be described as a sense of personal value and positive self-approval. Self-esteem is a recognition of your identity and is characterized by a sense of approval of your role in life as being significant. Positive self-regard is healthy. It is absolutely vital for every person. A damaged self-image, such as extreme feelings of inferiority or guilt, can disable a person as gravely as does paralysis. If you are having difficulty with your image of self, you need to memorize 2 Corinthians 9:8 and 11. It is both interesting and significant to note that there are seven superlatives listed in these two scriptural references alone!

*"And God is able to make **all** grace abound toward you; that ye **always** having **all** sufficiency in **all** things, may abound to **every** good work ... Being enriched in **every**thing to all bountifulness, which causeth through us thanksgiving to God."*

Unlike self-esteem, pride is a deadly disease. It is the only disease known to mankind which makes everyone else sick except the person who has it. It can be defined as an inordinate preoccupation with self and its processes. It is an undue self- veneration based upon unrealistic values.

In reality, pride is self-deification, which is a form of idolatry. Pride carries with it destructive characteristics, many of which are contrary to each other, such as:

1. SELF-DECEPTION

In self-deception an individual fails to recognize the cause and effect of his behaviour. Despite his despicable actions, and in the face of overwhelming evidence, Hitler actually deluded himself into thinking he was doing God's will by exterminating millions of human beings. Though on a much lesser scale, all prideful individuals labour under deception. Jeremiah stated that, "*The heart is deceitful above all things, and desperately wicked: who can know it?*" (Jeremiah 17:9) Because the proud person refuses to measure his actions against acceptable standards, his world of reality is limited to his subjective impressions. The Apostle Paul warned against this very thing when he explained: "*Let no man deceive himself.*" (1 Corinthians 3:18) For this reason, prideful people make poor business partners!

2. DENIAL

This person refuses to accept his limitations. He ignores responsibility and accountability for his actions and projects the blame for the unacceptable results of his actions onto someone or something else. Prideful people have much difficulty in accepting correction, instruction or constructive criticism. They usually assume a superior posture which is closely akin to vanity or conceit. They display a "know it all" attitude and seek to be in charge of every situation. "I'll have it my way!" is their theme song. In reality these poor people are struggling with horrendous feelings of inadequacy and they are continuously seeking to affirm themselves by being right. For obvious reasons, prideful people make poor employees!

3. SELF-CONSCIOUSNESS

A prideful person is painfully aware of himself. He is preoccupied with how he looks, feels and acts. How others see him is fearfully important to him, therefore his actions and motivations are predicted upon peer approval. When this is not forthcoming, he withdraws from competitive relationships. Such individuals find it difficult to accept help from others, lest they be seen as inadequate. They also find it difficult to share, since what is given may not be appreciated to the level of their expectation. To cloak these uneasy feelings, they garb themselves with a mantle of exaggerated independence. The catch-phrase goes something like this: "I don't need you! Get away! I can do it without any help!" It is evident that such folk make poor marriage partners!

4. SELF-GRATIFICATION

The satisfaction which is gained from self-esteem is often substituted by self-gratification. Every organism moves toward satisfaction. If you doubt this, try fasting for three days! Denying yourself of life's pleasures is painful. Satisfaction is an important dynamic, but must be derived from healthy sources. Self-esteem provides the satisfaction of well-being. When this is lacking, gratification is sought as an alternative. Usually this is done through physical and emotional indulgence. This is the primary reason for the popularity of the "night spots". It's not a matter of "drinking away your troubles," "eating because I'm hungry" or "finding new and exciting things to do." It is rather a futile attempt to fill the void with gratification. Every over-indulgence is gratification. Such people find discipline difficult. These people make poor friends.

5. SELF-CONDEMNATION

Self-condemnation is closely related to self-recrimination, self-abasement and self-devaluation. It is commonly known as "cratoring": a capitulation, a giving up, and a giving in to self-blame. These feelings of worthlessness can be so overwhelming that no other alternative but suicide is apparent. Although seldom acknowledged, suicide is spawned in a heart of pride. There can be no better illustration of this fact than to study the life of Saul, the first King of Israel. His life began in humility, rose to greatness and ended in ignominious defeat. His entire life was characterized by self-centred gratification.

"And Samuel said, When thou wast little in thine own sight, wast thou not made the head of the tribes of Israel, and the Lord anointed thee king over Israel? ... Behold, to obey is better than sacrifice, and to hearken than the fat of rams. For rebellion is as the sin of witchcraft, and stubbornness is as iniquity and idolatry. Because thou hast rejected the word of the Lord, he hath also rejected thee from being king."
- 1 Samuel 15:17, 22-23

Had Saul submitted himself to the wise counsel of Samuel, the outcome of his life would have been far different. You will find the narrative of his attempted suicide and shameful death in 1 Samuel 28-31. Help is available to those who submit themselves to wise counsel. People who reject discerning admonishment, make poor neighbours.

6. SELF-LOVE (NARCISSISM)

When individuals feel insufficiently loved, they tend to love themselves. This lavishing of your own love upon yourself is known as ego-centricity. Such people are preoccupied with their own concerns and are insensitive to the needs of others. They have a great deal of difficulty in their marriage and family relationships. They make poor parents.

A healthy self-esteem is based upon the spiritual aspect of what Jesus Christ has done for us. We are what we are because of His grace. Solomon's treatise on pride is crisp and clear:

"A man's pride shall bring him low: but honour shall uphold the humble in spirit." - Proverbs 29:23

This is one key to successful living!

KEY 34   WHAT YOU EAT IS WHAT YOU GET

The entire universe is governed by laws. So accurate and consistent are these laws, that man has formulated them into equations and constructed machines to utilize their powers. The law of gravity, for example, dictates that a falling object accelerates at the rate of 32 feet (approximately 10 m) per second. So constant is the pull of gravity that man never has to fear that he will fall off the earth. Another law was discovered by Daniel Bernoulli (1700-1782) which stated that: "As the velocity of the fluid increases, the pressure in the fluid decreases." Knowing these laws, aero-engineers have configured the wings of an aircraft in such a manner as to balance lift against gravity, enabling man to fly. Ignorance of these laws would have kept the majority of us walking.

Another example is the law of chemistry. When two molecules of hydrogen are united with one molecule of oxygen, water is formed. Automobile manufacturers could use this law to rid every city of its smog, if they could develop an engine that burns hydrogen. Hydrogen burns as a clean efficient fuel with pure water as its only residue. The laws of thermodynamics state that water freezes at 32 and boils at 212 degrees Fahrenheit (0 and 100 degrees Celcius), a simple formula which will determine whether I take my skis to the mountains or my suntan lotion to the beach. Astronomers look forward with keen anticipation to the next arrival of Haley's comet. Because the laws of astronomy are consistent, they can determine with pin-point accuracy the time and place of its arrival every 76 years.

When the laws which govern the universe and life around us are violated, the consequences can be devastating. Ignorance of these laws cannot make us immune to the effects of breaking them. The example of gravity is clear. Whether you understand the law of gravity, and whether you believe it or not, will make no difference to the way you will be going when you step outside of a 30 story window. Any violation of these principles will produce ill effects. It is a sobering thought, but true, that the burden of responsibility for success or failure rests on the individual's doorstep!

This is not a dissertation on "Sickness, its causes and cures." However, we would all benefit by understanding some of the dynamics which aid well-being. The greatest business in the world today is health care. More money is spent on hospitalization, medication, surgery, cures, remedies and carnival cure-all snake oil than on national defence. As in the days of the Greeks, physical well-being has become a nation-wide pursuit. Fear of pain, suffering and sickness has become a major preoccupation.

Before a cure can be effective, the cause of the problem must be determined. All of life is governed by the dynamics which exist between cause and effect. If the cause can be determined and altered, then a change can be effected.

Infection can be a major cause of sickness. Immunology is the science which deals with the nature and cause of immunity from diseases. It is known that the body has the ability to reject infection. This is a major obstacle to organ transplants. A healthy body rejects most foreign matter. The common cold which is a minor annoyance to most people, is a lethal infection to the aborigines in non-developed lands. This is true because they have never developed an immunity to the virus. Simple precautions such as washing hands or sneezing into a handkerchief make good health sense. Cleanliness and personal hygiene are important.

In the book of Deuteronomy God established many health rules which were designed to ensure well-being for the children of Israel. One of the instructions is found in chapter 23:12-13. Please do not be offended by its explicit clarity.

"Thou shalt have a place also without the camp, whither thou shalt go forth abroad: And thou shalt have a paddle upon thy weapon; and it shall be, when thou wilt ease thyself abroad, thou shalt dig therewith, and shalt turn back and cover that which cometh from thee."

In simple modern day language, they were instructed to "flush the toilet" every time they used it. And for good reason. Those who travel in under-developed countries tell stories of communities which have no refuse control. Sewage runs openly in the street. Its foul smell breeds more than flies, mosquitoes and rodents. Infection runs rampant and with it a high mortality rate. During the days of Jesus, there was a high degree of blindness in Samaria. The Samaritans were a cross-breed people, the offspring of mixed marriages between the Israelites and members of occupying forces and peoples of other tribes who were unsympathetic to these laws. They lived in disobedience to these regulations. No importance was placed on these commandments. Human sewage, household swill and animal refuse ran openly in the streets. The evaporation processes would free the infection and toxins which were eliminated from the body by the digestive systems. These were then carried by wind, insects and body contact back to the people. How sad! Countless people lived in darkness and were ravaged by diseases. Untold millions died unnecessarily and prematurely, and all because they violated a simple Biblical principle of hygiene.

What is or is not eaten, also plays a major role in sickness and in health. The World Book Dictionary defines the word *ingest* in this way: "to take (food, etc.) into the body for digestion. To take in; accommodate." Many scientists now believe that the major reason for many of our physical illnesses is our eating habits. Americans suffer more coronaries and strokes than any other culture. They believe it is because we are the best fed people on earth. We are killing ourselves with our table ware.

If it is true that we are what we eat, then it is wise to assess what we eat in terms of time, place, amount and kind. Most Americans don't eat to live. They live to eat. And why not? Food is available to us in abundance, prepared in countless ways and served to us in any way pleasure may demand. In effect, what we are doing is digging our graves with our knives and forks. The very blessing of our affluence has become our curse.

1. OVER-EATING

Over-eating does more than deposit fat on the abdomen and hips. It forms cholesterol plaques on the insides of the blood vessels, greatly restricting blood flow. This causes excessive strain on the heart. Over-eating is a form of suicide on an instalment plan! Life insurance companies rate premiums according to your weight, knowing that your expected life span is directly related to it.

2. FOOD PRESERVATION AND PREPARATION

Much of the food we eat is so highly processed, chemically prepared and preserved, that it is harmful to the consumer. This fact is illustrated by the following quotation from the Republic Scene, October 1981. It was written by Dennis Meredith and titled: *How Science Keeps A Chicken In Every Pot.*

"... there is no such thing as a "chicken" any more. There are only mass-produced, computer-monitored, antibiotic-treated, protein-producing biological units. ... in its eight-week life span, the average broiler receives at least twenty antibiotics, minerals and vitamins to make it grow faster and to protect it from the myriad of diseases that are the chicken's lot ... So, there are penicillin and neoterramycine to stimulate growth and improve the efficiency of feed utilization. There are tetracycline to protect against respiratory diseases, sinusitis, bluecomb, hexamitiasis, synovitis and coccidiosis. There is oxytetracycline to protect against fowl cholera and avian infectious hepatitis. There are nitrofuran to protect against fowl typhoid, pullorum, airsac infection and ulcerative enteritis. There is ethoxyquin to guard against encphalomalocia. And there are arsenate compounds to stimulate growth and give the skin that delicious yellow colouring."

The meat processors then dissect the chicken for the pot, preserving the pieces with chlorides, salts and phosphates. Further steps are taken to ensure that trichinosis, salmonella or botulism do not breed. They are then shipped and stored for undetermined lengths of time in uncontrolled environments. When a hungry diner orders his meal, the specified portions of "biologically produced protein units" are then deep fried in animal fat and served as a tantalizing delicacy. Oh yes, let's not forget the salt which is liberally applied for seasoning.

The foods we eat are not poisonous, but an unwise and prolonged diet of certain preserved and highly processed foods can be harmful. The fact that we are still alive, attests to God's protective mercies!

3. KINDS OF FOOD

The words "ingestive materials", would be a better way to describe some of the food we eat. It would be best to stay completely away from such. W C Fields jokingly alluded to his eating custom when he said: "Some scoundrel stole the cork from my lunch." Alcohol is neither a food nor a drink. It is called a beverage only because it can be swallowed as a liquid. But so can battery acid and Draino.

4. TIME

Meals eaten at noon can be worked off during the day's activity. Late meals tend to lie in the stomach and then to transfer to the hips. A good rule to follow is this: Eat like a potentate (king) for breakfast, like a peasant for lunch, and like a pauper for supper.

God gave the children of Israel a set of dietary laws. Most of them are found in Leviticus 11 and Deuteronomy 14. They were warned that the diseases of the heathen nations would befall those who disregarded these laws. The cause for sickness was established in order to prevent it.

God gave them their **don't** and confirmed His reason with **because,** a cause and effect formula!

"... whereof thou canst not be healed." - *Deuteronomy 28:27, 35*

They were also told that if they kept the laws, none of the diseases which other nations suffered would befall them.

"And said, If thou wilt diligently hearken to the voice of the Lord thy God, and wilt do that which is right in his sight, and wilt give ear to his commandments, and keep all his statutes, I will put none of these diseases upon thee, which I have brought upon the Egyptians: for **I am the Lord that healeth thee** *(Jehovah- Rapha)."* - *Exodus 15:26*

The human body is a marvellous machine, as described by King David in Psalm 139:14: *"... I am fearfully and wonderfully made ..."* It is one of a kind and the only machine like it you will ever have on earth. Take good care of it. The owner of an automobile would never put sand, salt, sugar, water, tobacco or other harmful materials into his fuel tank. These elements may be useful for other applications, but not in the fuel tank! He secures the gas cap every time he fills the tank. This he does to prevent dust or dirt from entering the gas-lines. It might be a good idea to make such a plug for our mouths to help us resist the temptation of ingesting the harmful. Either that, or else courage, determination and discipline to stop.

This is one key to successful living!

KEY 35   POOR CHARLIE!

I once attended the funeral of a close friend who was well respected and honoured on state level for his contribution to the community. Single-handedly, he had built one of the finest programs and facilities for drug and alcohol rehabilitation. Despite his accomplishments and broad recognition, he had few friends. He was often criticized for his inflexibility, bullheadedness, bluntness and narrowness of mind.

The church was filled with people who lined up for two hours to pay their last respects. The air was heavy with the scent of flowers, tired ceiling high. Eulogies were offered by the mayor, state representatives and clergymen from several denominations, all extolling his determination, tenacity, forthrightness and singleness of purpose! "Farewell to a good man, a friend of the community," read the caption in the news release.

As I listened to the words spoken over his casket, I pondered the privilege which was mine to have known him and for having the honour to have worked with him. "Poor Charlie," I thought, "too bad he isn't here to benefit from all this!" My next thought was, "Lucky Charlie! He doesn't have to witness the emptiness and fickleness of this insincere charade." While he was alive, he was bitterly criticized as being inflexible. Now he is exalted for his determination. He was opposed as being bullheaded, blunt and lacking in tact. Now he is characterized as having tenacity and forthrightness. His narrowness is now hailed as singleness of purpose. Friendless during life, he now has a reception line an hour long, to tell him how pleased they were to have known him. Eulogy followed eulogy, extolling Charlie's virtues. The pious platitudes reeked with repugnance!

"Where was this entourage when he was building the rehabilitation centre single-handedly?" I thought. "Where was this good-will, this support, when he needed it?" I stood by his widow and grieved, but not for Charlie. Somewhere love and honour and kindness and ethics and selflessness had died. This was not a remembrance service in honour of a great man. At best it was a disgraceful parade of "Whose Who" in the absence of integrity. At its worst, it was the genocide of every synonym which may describe the honour and dignity of mankind! It was as though authenticity had died, and with it also respect for others. But even worse, the vast majority of those in attendance were unaware of its passing. As painful as the experience was, I learned some valuable lessons:

1. SHOW YOUR KINDNESS NOW

The present is the best time to give your verbal bouquets. I determined to give my flowers to those who are alive and can enjoy them now. "Here, I brought this over for you. I thought you might have some use for it!" or, "I was in the store today and I thought of you. I hope you enjoy this little gift!" I resolved that such phrases would characterize my speech.

2. HELP SOMEONE TODAY

Now is the time to give a helping hand to those in need. I determined to give my support where it could benefit someone. "I see you working hard. May I help you?" or, "Here, let me go with you. We will get it done twice as fast if two of us work at it." I pledged that these attitudes would be evident in my being.

3. SPEAK WORDS OF ENCOURAGEMENT

Speech must always be encouraging and edifying to others. I determined to express my appreciation where and when it could be a source of encouragement. "You did that well! You are a real pleasure to me." "I genuinely appreciate the way you do or say that." I promised to tell someone something like that every day.

4. TOUCH SOMEONE WITH LOVE

Reach out and touch someone with appreciation today. I determined to take time and pay my respects when both parties could benefit. "Charlie, are you free tonight? Come over for coffee. My wife makes a 'smashing' cake!" "Let's get together for breakfast." "Can I pick you up?" I committed myself to hospitality and to reach out to those around me.

It takes little effort or personal cost to pay your last respects to the deceased. Remember, even a tombstone can say something nice about the "guy that's down!" Your determination to show your respects to those who can benefit from it will cost you in terms of time, effort, inconvenience and money. But when you do this, you encourage and enhance the lives of those around you, and you write your own eulogies in the epitaphs of the hearts of men.

On Remembrance Day I undertook to write an essay in honour of those who had influenced my life. I had planned to spend four hours in deep recollection and thanksgiving, honouring those who had contributed positively to my development. I began with fervour and gratitude.

The list included my parents, who despite their poverty, loved me, encouraged me, and always kept me clothed and well fed; a public school friend who played long hours with me; a high school principal who sat and cried when he told me of his decision to expel me for bad behaviour; a college buddy who would defend me with his honour; several professors who patiently instructed me and endured my failures; the missionary couple who led me to Jesus; my beloved companion who faithfully walked with me for more than three decades on our way to "happily for ever after"; a few more, and certainly Charlie, dear Charlie!

My essay abruptly stopped 30 minutes later, with the startling discovery of how few entries I had made. Countless people have walked across the stage of my life. The overwhelming majority passed into total oblivion, without having made one single contribution to the person I am today! I was astonished with how pitifully few people have been a positive force in my life. At that point I made a quality decision for my life. I determined to give positive regard to those around me; to encourage others with my speech and influence; to take time to help someone who may be in need; and to daily touch someone with my appreciation! It would do us all well to heed the scriptural instruction in Romans 13:7-8:

> *"Render therefore to all their dues: tribute to whom tribute is due; custom to whom custom; fear to whom fear; honour to whom honour. Owe no man any thing, but to love one another: for he that loveth another hath fulfilled the law."*

This is one key to successful living!

KEY 36   VERBAL JOUSTING

The medieval sport of jousting was a popular sport and an essential military exercise during the days of chivalry. Dressed in full armour and mounted on their steeds, knights would meet at opposite ends of a field. A damsel would officially begin the game by dropping a lady's scarf to the ground. The knights would charge toward each other in a cloud of dust and thundering hooves. With pinpointed accuracy they honed in on each other with lance or club or swinging ball and chain. The game would end a few seconds later in the centre of the field, with a collision and an explosion of metal fragments, dust and assorted debris. When the air cleared and the fall-out settled, a winner was declared. The winner was easily identified. It was he who still had his head and brains intact! Both had lost. Both emerged battle-scarred, both bled, both suffered agonizing pain, both would need weeks to recuperate. None the less, the winner was declared, namely he who bled least. It seems crude and barbaric to our cultured, highly-literate, twentieth century society. "Imagine that!" said one socialite, "A sport where grown people beat each other half to death. How brutish!"

As primitive as jousting may be, this is exactly what happens in the modern game of **verbal jousting**. Domestic squabbles, family furore, household blow-outs, marital torque-out or parental blow-up, call it what you wish, but domestic fighting is the police officer's greatest fear.

Eighty percent of all homicides take place within a domestic setting. Not all arguments end in physical violence, but verbal battles are equally destructive. The emotional pain and psychological scarring which spouses inflict upon each other, are far more painful and injurious than physical brutality. Wounds heal quickly, but a bruised self-image, broken hopes, shattered plans, broken vows, rejected confidences and broken spirits are not easily mended. A familiar adage disregards the serious nature of interpersonal strife with these words:

> Sticks and stones
> May break my bones,
> But names will never hurt me!

This proverb is not only naive and erroneous, but also dangerously harmful. Sticks and stones may break your bones, but they will heal in the process of time. Abrasions, lacerations and contusions are severe, but they will mend! The emotional and mental scarring which takes place as a result of violence and brutality, however, may take decades to heal. In most cases the individual is emotionally stained and scarred for life. Apart from the intervening grace of the Great Physician, there will be no healing!

How frequently have you heard the following damaging statements made in heated argument? "You fool! You idiot! That's ridiculous! You're a loud-mouthed aggressive ...! You are ugly and stupid!" Such verbal interchange is as barbaric as the medieval "sport" of jousting!

It is possible, however, that you are one of the rare people who are not interested in civilized interchange. Perhaps you enjoy the barbarism of verbal jousting. If you are, here are twenty winning moves that will enable you to prove your point, get your way, and win the game. A word of caution must also be noted. If these moves become your life-style, you run the risk of being fired from your job, finding yourself friendless, or losing your marriage partner and your family. If getting your own way and proving your point are important to you, then these moves will surely improve your chances of winning.

TWENTY WINNING MOVES FOR VERBAL JOUSTING:

- Get him where it hurts!
- Let her have it!
- Yell real loud!
- Remind him of his failures!
- Compare her to some frump!
- Shout something disrespectful!
- Tell her she is like her family!
- Declare him a total failure!
- Tell her she has never met your needs!
- Spit at him!
- Blurt out some shocking obscenity!
- Slam the door!
- Throw something, like dishes!
- Destroy his prized possession!
- Clam up. Use the cold silent treatment!
- Cry a lot!
- Run home to Mamma. Go stay with the boys!
- Get high, real smashed!
- Disappear for three days!
- Sleep on the couch!
- ... and more!

Who wins in this sick game? **No one!** You both lose! These may be common moves used for verbal jousting, but they are not winning moves. You may have overpowered or out-shouted your "opponent", you may have succeeded in getting your way, but both of you have lost! Lost is peace, self-respect, dignity, honour, laughter, a good meal, a peaceful night's sleep, a happy spouse, a happy family and a well-adjusted disposition. The price paid for playing the game of verbal jousting, is exceedingly high.

Solomon, who is acknowledged as the wisest man who has ever lived, gives us a move which guarantees a win. It is found in the Book of Proverbs:

"A soft answer turneth away wrath (anger): but grievous words stir up anger." - Proverbs 15:1

Remember: Anger is one letter short of danger!
            D + anger = danger!

To joust or not to joust, that is the question. To stay and fight in a domestic setting should not be seen as macho, but as weakness and barbaric. Any horse can kick, any dog can bark, any carnivore can rip, tear and chew. It takes a person of maturity and strength to show restraint. People of character are able to control their emotions and work through each problem. Here are a few helpful manoeuvres for winning the game of domestic bliss. They are rightly called "Winning Moves!"

TWENTY WINNING MOVES FOR DOMESTIC BLISS:

- Delay discussion until you have cooled off, real cool!
- Avoid derogatory statements!
- Address the issue!
- Abstain from remembering the other's personal weaknesses!
- Refrain from bizarre, irrational behaviour!
- Talk in subdued tones!
- Listen to what the other person is saying!
- Ignore tone of voice and inflection of expression!
- Avoid blanket statements like, "You always..."
- Don't project blame!
- Assume your share of the responsibility!
- Don't resist the need for change!
- Accept responsibility and accountability!
- Try doing something else other than arguing together!
- Divert your interests to more pleasant things!
- Give deference to the other. Prefer one another!
- Learn to say, "I'm sorry! Please forgive me!"
- Display a teachable attitude!
- Don't worry, be happy!
- Pray together about the problem. It beats jousting!

It is recommended that before you begin your game of Verbal Jousting, the participants sit down together and study the rules of the game as contained in James 3:13-18:

"Who is a wise man and endued with knowledge among you? Let him shew out of a good conversation his works with meekness of wisdom. But if ye have bitter envying and strife in your hearts, glory not, and lie not against the truth. This wisdom descendeth not from above, but is earthly, sensual, devilish. For where envying and strife is, there is confusion and every evil work. But the wisdom that is from above is first pure, then peaceable, full of mercy and good fruits, without partiality and without hypocrisy. And the fruit of righteousness is sown in peace of them that make peace."

This is one key to successful living!

KEY 37   INCOMPATIBILITY OR INFLEXIBILITY

When he discovered my profession, the passenger beside me sought to engage me in conversation. I was en route to a speaking engagement and was trying to put the finishing touches to my remarks. He asked, "How important is compatibility in a marriage? You see, I'm thinking of marriage and am wondering if I can adjust to the relationship compatibly?" Thinking this to be a sincere and thought-provoking question, I put my study aside and tried to answer his query. After a few moments of conversation he said, "Well, you see, I'm living with this girl, and I kind of think I'm tired of her, and I don't know how to drop her. You see, I made some promises to her ... I really don't think I'm compatible with her!" Like a flash of lightning it dawned on me that he wasn't interested in discussing compatibility at all. All he wanted was to satisfy his sexual drives without accountability or responsibility to anyone, and after having done so, to cast aside the relationship without feeling guilty about destroying his partner. It was not direction or understanding he was looking for, he merely wanted attention and an accomplice. He was asking for my approval of his questionable behaviour.

The majority of people who ask for counsel are not looking for direction. They are wanting attention or an accomplice - someone to agree with them!

Looking directly at him I responded, "I'm not too sure I understand your question. If it is incompatibility that we are talking about, I see it the same as I see inflexibility. And inflexibility is the offspring of self-gratifying selfishness!" I then related the illustration found in Matthew 19:3-8. The story is told of the Pharisees who sought to entrap Jesus by asking him this subtle question: "*Is it lawful for a man to put away his wife for every cause?*" Their motive was ulterior! They didn't want to know the answer. All they wanted, was to trap Jesus in heresy. Jesus told them that according to the Law of Moses, which they knew well, it was God who joined them in marriage. Therefore, let no mere man break them apart! To this they responded with legal jurisdiction, "*Why did Moses then command to give a writing of divorcement, and to put her away?*" Jesus' response was classic:

"*Moses because of the hardness of your hearts suffered you to put away your wives: but from the beginning it was not so.*"

After a moment's pause I added, "If you understand self-gratifying selfishness and its outcome, which is "hard heartedness", then you will understand the meaning of incompatibility!"

Here are some characteristics of compatibility and its antithesis:

1. PATIENCE

Patience can endure inconvenience and provocation. It gives no place for resentment or revenge. Long-suffering overlooks life's many slights, and seeks positive effects. Irritating impatience is a sure sign of self-centredness. It can only lead to incompatibility.

2. KINDNESS

Kindness looks for opportunities to exercise thoughtfulness. It is helpful, solicitous and nurturing. It welcomes an occasion to make a meaningful contribution to someone or something else. Self-gratifying indulgence, however, is kind to self, even at another's expense.

3. NON-ENVIOUS

Compatibility is happy to see the success and satisfaction of others. It is not jealous or grieved because of the good fortune of someone else. Incompatibility is bloated with self-indulgence, and is preoccupied with personal satisfaction.

4. NOT BOASTFUL

A compatible person is quick to complement someone on a job well done. He seeks occasion to say something positive about someone else. A boastful person seeks to bring attention to himself and is soon deceived by flattery. Boastfulness is tantamount to ego-centredness.

5. HUMBLE

A compatible person is able to accept a compliment but does not engage in conceit, neither does he display false humility which epitomises inadequacy. Pride is mere self-exaltation. It worships at its own cenotaph, a form of self-deification.

6. IMPERTURBABLE

Compatible people are not easily agitated. They conduct themselves with courtesy and goodwill regardless of circumstances. Rudeness is inconsiderate of the other's feelings. When perturbed, incomparible people respond according to their whims and urges, regardless of those around them.

7. FORGIVING

Compatible people never seek to placate personal desires at the expense or the hurt of others. They quickly overlook annoyances and forgive those who have wronged them. Bitterness keeps a record of wrongs done against it, and seeks an opportunity for vengeance.

8. HAPPY IN TRUTH

A compatible person harbours no malice. He functions according to a set standard of ethics and morals and is quick to discern right from wrong. Truth is not afraid to expose the hidden secret things. Its hallmark is openness. Self-centredness will protect itself with lies, insinuations and innuendos.

9. PROTECTIVE OF OTHERS

Compatible people wish no ill to anyone. They do not take delight in the misfortunes of others. They will take no part in doing mischief or harm. The rights and privileges of others, however, is no concern of the self-centred.

10. TRUSTWORTHY AND ACCEPTING

A compatible person takes no pleasure in publishing the shortcomings and faults of another. They loathe to expose another's misfortunes or to display his deficiencies. The self- seeking find it difficult to trust or accept others, primarily because they themselves cannot be trusted.

Self is at the root of most interpersonal stresses. When you are self-complying it is difficult to be flexible. Meeting the other person's needs requires a great deal of personal effort and yielding. Concession and demand is the price to be paid for compatibility. It is a price that garners great dividends! Paul's great discourse to the Corinthians on the subject of love, is a university course on **compatibility!**

"And now I will show you the most excellent way. If I speak in the tongues of men and of angels, but have not love, I am only a resounding gong or a clanging cymbal. If I have the gift of prophecy and can fathom all mysteries and all knowledge, and if I have a faith that can move mountains, but have not love, I am nothing. If I give all I possess to the poor and surrender my body to the flames, but have not love, I gain nothing. Love is patient, love is kind. It does not envy, it does not boast, it is not proud. It is not rude, it is not self-seeking, it is not easily

angered, it keeps no record of wrongs. Love does not delight in evil but rejoices with the truth. It always protects, always trusts, always hopes, always perseveres. Love never fails." - 1 Corinthians13:1-8 (New International Version)

This is one key to successful living!

KEY 38   MARRIAGE CAN BE A PAIN

With broad smiles and excitement radiating from their eyes, a young couple proudly announced, "We are engaged! We would like you to perform the wedding. Could you do that for us?" After extending congratulations and affirming my willingness to work with them, I warned: "Marriage is a real pain in the neck, you know! If you want to be spared a lot of trouble, your best bet is to stay single!" "Surely, you must be jesting? Aren't you?" they responded. "No, indeed!" I replied.

Marriage at best is a concession and a demand!

As blissful as the married state can be, it is none the less a concession and a demand! If two are going to live as "one flesh", both partners must be willing to compromise and to submit to the roles that marriage and parenthood demand! It is for this reason that the Apostle Paul penned the following warning:

> *"Are you married? Do not seek a divorce. Are you unmarried? Do not look for a wife. But if you do marry, you have not sinned; and if a virgin marries, she has not sinned. But those who marry will face many troubles in this life, (trouble in the flesh - King James Version) and I want to spare you this." - 1 Corinthians 7:27-28 (New International Version)*

Here are several obvious causes which can make marriage a "trouble in the flesh" or a "pain in the neck".

1. EGO-CENTREDNESS AND SELF-PROMOTION

The ego-centred person thinks in the singular. His choices are expressed in the singular pronoun: "I will retire early this evening! I think I'll watch the football game! I will go up town tonight and have a bowl of clam chowder!" A single person may be excused for this kind of thought-process, since the damage done is primarily to self. A married person must think in plurality. "Tonight, **we** will watch the football game!" More often than not, this assertion is made much more timidly: "Honey, do you think we can watch the football game tonight?" When the family begins to arrive, the married person must think corporately. A self-centred person is unable to think in plurality or corporately. Thinking patterns for the married person must move from the singular, through the plural, to a corporate configuration.

Most couples entering marriage know this. It is evident that a selfish or ego-centric person is disqualified as a good spouse or family person. The change from singular through plural, to corporate thinking can be very traumatic and time-consuming. Mature people adjust quickly.

2. TWO PEOPLE LIVING AS ONE BODY

Two people living as one can be crowding and disjointing. The physical differences between a man and a woman are obvious. Those who fail to see them, need not read any further! The differences in personality and character are even greater. When the bride and groom enter their honeymoon suit for the first time, it is done with great anticipation. This is their first night together on their way to *forever happily ever after!* To their horror they discover that their parents are in bed with them. Indeed, from both sides of the family! The person you married is not just a warm body. No, you married a family, an ethnic origin, a life-style, and all the characteristics which go into the making of a person. Our developmental years, known as our rearing and background, determine our values, tastes, modes of operation, orientation, interests and much more. These are only a few of the components which make up personality. Frequently a husband and wife will find themselves at cross purposes with each other and pulling in opposite directions, simply because they have different goals and motivations.

Such stresses can be called *functional disorders*. It is simply a matter of learning how to function efficiently with each other. Mature people know how to bend. They do not see their yielding to their mate's desires as a weakness. They do not object to the bending process, nor do they perceive it as abandoning their identity. They willingly give deference to the other. However, such bending is painful to the ego.

3. I'M RIGHT AND I'LL HAVE IT MY WAY ATTITUDE

Personality differences can be very irritating. After all, the way I have been doing it is the correct way! Is it? Perhaps this is why so many people enter marriage with this mind-set:

I'll alter Walter,
When I have him
By the halter,
At the altar!

How does the expedient, slipshod personality type affect the detailed, compulsive type? How does the shy, inhibited person affect the venturesome, uninhibited and socially bold person? How does the relaxed, calm person live with the tense, driven and overwrought character? The answer: With much difficulty!

Like opposite polls of a magnet, opposites often attract. The shy person may have a great admiration for the overt, outgoing type. Never being able to express himself with self-assuring confidence, he vicariously finds assertion in his spouse. Now he can be dominant and competitive in the world he lives. On the other hand, she has always desired to be gentle, soft-spoken and retiring, and finds in him, her counterpart. Unfortunately, the very factors which drew them together, quickly become the very dynamics which drive them apart. He soon sees her as being aggressive, dominant, forward and unyielding. He is unable to compete with her assertiveness, he withdraws from competitiveness. She sees him as a weak, docile and easily led wimp.

Mature people recognize their partner's differences, yet accept them right where they are! They seek to accommodate and complement the other. They are quick to recognize the other's strong characteristics and to overlook the weak. They are patient with the other. And yet, such long-suffering can be loooong suffering!

Marriage can be beautiful, but it takes maturity and effort on both sides. That is why marriage is for adults and not for children. It is surprising how many older folk are still acting like children. Here is a simple prayer for maturity. It would do us all well to pray it:

> "Lord Jesus, help me to entreat my spouse with maturity. Help me to be slow to see his/her weak points and quick to see his/her strong characteristics. Help me to complement him/her on his/her successes and to overlook his/her failures. May I be patient in my dealings with him/her, always being sensitive to his/her needs. Increase my love for him/her and help me to display this in my daily relationships with him/her. Give me Your strength Lord, to be an ever improving help-mate!"

In a small cemetery just beyond the limits of the city of Kelowna, British Columbia, Canada, a tombstone gives mute testimony to a successful marriage. Inscribed on the headstone are written these words:

> This happy marriage of 54 years,
> was built through many sacrifices!

This is one key to successful living!

KEY 39   LOVE IS A DECISION

He was cold, metallic and indifferent. "I don't love you any more! I have lost all my feelings towards you, and I just don't care", he said. Then he added, "There is nothing I can do about it. That's the way it is!" She was devastated. His wife sat sobbing uncontrollably and with no verbal response. After all, what was left to say? Seventeen years of caring, of trying, of effort, and what for? What a tragedy! Seventeen years in the making, the endless hours of personal effort on both parts; the memories both good and bad; the relationships which were established; the sharing; the things they did together, now all is about to be lost! Note the basis on which the decision was made:

* I don't love you any more!
* I don't have any feelings for you!
* There is nothing I can do about it!
* That's the way it is!

A cursory analysis of his statements reveals the erroneous basis upon which his decision was made, and the delusion under which he operated. It also points to the true character of his nature and motives.

1. I DON'T LOVE YOU ANY MORE

His statement, "I don't love you any more!" presupposes a choice. In actual fact, what he was saying was: "I don't choose to love you any more!" Love is a matter of will. As a person, I make the choice whom I shall love and to what degree. The basis upon which we determine our love may be poorly determined and ill-defined. The reasons for choice vary widely, and differ as broadly as do our faces. Choice is also subject to change. This fact is supported by his statement: "I don't love you **any more** !" There are many contingencies which go into the making of choice, but it is a certainty that love is a matter of will. Love is a condition of the will. Love is a decision. Love is a choice.

2. I DON'T HAVE ANY FEELINGS FOR YOU

The assertion, "I don't have any feelings for you!" indicates that a choice had been made, and that this choice had affected his emotions. Feelings or emotions are the outcome of choice. Emotions are as many and as variegated as the hues of a sunset. They are the oils of life which highlight the grey canvasses of daily mundane tedium. The emotional colours with which you paint is a matter of choice. That choice will determine the value of the portrait. Will your brush strokes bring delight to those who view your painting, or will it lie in the attic dust of broken promises and discarded memories?

Emotion is that distinct human quality which makes people superior to pinion pine trees. I suppose that this is one reason why men prefer kissing ladies as opposed to trees. It must be noted that feeling is a dynamic which can be controlled. Intense hate, preoccupying bitterness, overwhelming fear, raging anger, driving passion and other feelings can be subdued. The direction and intensity of emotion are direct consequences of choice. Feelings are therefore controllable, replaceable and dismissable! If this were not true, it would invalidate many scriptural admonitions which have given strength to many people, for example:

- *Rejoice, and again I say rejoice!*
- *Let not your heart be troubled!*
- *The joy of the Lord shall be your strength!*
- *Be not afraid!*
- *Be of good courage!*

3. I CAN'T DO ANYTHING ABOUT IT

The conclusion, "I can't do anything about it!" is completely in error. "Certainly, you can!" I challenged him. "The question is do you want to? Is it worth the effort? Is the trauma which the choice will cause greater than the discomfort of trying once again?" Every person is able to do much about his feelings and behaviour. You alone have the authority over your responses. You are not a puppet. You alone pull your emotional and behavioral strings. There is no need to respond to the tugging of random circumstances. It is a well-established principle that a course of action is pursued once a choice has been made. Each choice is predicted upon your concepts, values and social and spiritual norms. These are based upon the sensory information you received from the world around you. Once the mind concludes that, "I'm in love! I've fallen out of love! I'm angry! I'm depressed! Life is great and I'm glad to be alive!" acting upon it is automatic. Both actions and feelings fall in line with thinking!

It is certain that all behaviour is determined by a thought process! Solomon established this fact when he declared:

"For as he thinketh in his heart, so is he ..." - *Proverbs 23:7*

The book of James addresses this subject in no uncertain terms. Please note the development of the action:

"And remember, when someone wants to do wrong it is never God who is tempting him, for God never wants to do wrong and never tempts anyone else to do it. Temptation is the pull of man's own evil thoughts and wishes. These evil thoughts lead to evil actions and afterwards to

*the death penalty from God. So don't be misled, dear brothers." -
James 1:13-16 (The Living Bible)*

4. THAT'S THE WAY IT IS

This is a statement of finality. What he is saying is: "There is nothing, Nothing, **Nothing**, that can be said or done to alter my choice!" How foolish! Nothing in life is certain except death and taxes. That's the way it is! But everything else in life is subject to change and individual choice. Once again I challenged him: "You are like the man who said, *Don't confuse me with facts. My mind is made up!* If nothing can be said or done to influence your thinking, then your coming here is a total waste of time and effort. To continue our discussion is futile. If *That's the way it is,* continuing this relationship serves only to perpetuate your unhappiness."

Moses and Joshua give us better counsel:

> *"I call heaven and earth to record this day against you, that I have set before you life and death, blessing and cursing: therefore choose life, that both thou and thy seed may live." - Deuteronomy 30:19*

> *"Now therefore fear the Lord, and serve him in sincerity and in truth ... And if it seem evil unto you to serve the Lord, choose you this day whom ye will serve ... but as for me and my house, we will serve the Lord." - Joshua 24:14-15*

This is one key to successful living!

KEY 40   REVERSALS CAN BE BENEFICIAL

Cliches are often used to immortalize a day or an event, for example: "The Blizzard of '82", "The December to Remember", "The Rain and Ice that Came!" and "The Big Blow!" These expressions aptly describe the extreme weather patterns which hit North America. A severe snow storm dumped four feet (approximately 1 m) of snow on Denver, Colorado, in a twenty four hour period, inundating the city with paralysing white. The entire population was under house-arrest for three days. It cost the city eight million dollars for snow removal and millions more in loss of business revenue. Unexpected events can be very traumatizing. One man suffered a coronary during the storm and because there was no way to get help to him, he died. His body lay in state in the garage for three days, waiting for the ambulance. Most inconveniences caused by unscheduled reversals are far less damaging, however.

In most cases, reversals produce many positive by-products. Many stories of kindness and heroism emerged, and people spoke fondly of the things they discovered during their trouble. Here are ten things which the inclement weather brought to those who *Remember December.*

1. IT ENCOURAGED HOSPITALITY

One city resident met his next door neighbour for the first time in three years. He was in desperate need of transportation and came to request a jump start to get his car going. Later that day they shared an evening meal together. Could this be the beginning of a new friendship?

2. IT PRODUCED DEFERENCE

A self-centred businessman who was never seen without his three piece pinstriped suit, donned a pair of snow boots and work clothes to shovel the walk-way of an elderly resident. There are many positive benefits which accrue from thinking about and doing for others. Could this be the very key which can set him free from his self-imposed prison of ego-centricity?

3. IT MOTIVATED SHARING

A lady who ran out of milk for her young one, was able to borrow the last quart (litre) from her neighbour. Giving from our abundance is tantamount to tipping a waitress. Giving from our lack or need, is giving of ourselves. Is there any benefit which can be derived from preferring others to ourselves?

4. IT ENHANCED COMMUNICATION

A husband and wife who were snowed in together were forced to discuss their irritations and differences with each other. They had lived together for seventeen years and this was their first meaningful conversation. How many problems did they avoid by such openness? What are the values of increased understanding?

5. IT DEVELOPED PARENTING SKILLS

Parents were locked in with their children. They were forced to read stories to the little ones, play family games and show home movies and colour slides of their past. The children had a ball! Rather than being "driven up the wall" by their constant presence, what can be learned from such close exchanges? What do you suppose they discovered when they played their game of Scrabble or Yahtsee over a cup of hot chocolate?

6. IT CLEARED AWAY ADMINISTRATIVE DUTIES

Overdue letters were written, household accounting was done, books were read and telephone calls were made. The basement and garage were cleaned and tools arranged in order. Sowing and mending were completed. What are the benefits of such "fence mending"?

7. IT PRODUCED CONGENIALITY

Expressions of encouragement, cheerful well-wishes and salutations were exchanged with others, even with total strangers. What are the by-products of such a cheerful disposition and positive mind-set?

8. IT AFFECTED HOME MAINTENANCE

Minor home repairs were made. My wife, Donna, was exceedingly happy with her husband because I had the time and motivation to wallpaper her bathroom. I can attest that we were both happy. She, because her bathroom was finally decorated, and I, because my nagging preoccupation to get it done had abated! Is there any benefit in doing something for someone that can make that someone happy?

9. IT PRODUCED CONTENTMENT

A new appreciation was gained for such simple things as a warm house, a car that would start, or water faucets that ran freely. We have become so sophisticated in our thinking that countless benefits have been taken for granted. Is there any benefit in taking time to count our many blessings?

10. IT GENERATED THANKSGIVING

While many complained, others were overwhelmed with gratitude for the benefits that were theirs. We live in an uncertain and unstable world. Any semblance of stability and certainty should be viewed with a grateful attitude.

Rarely do we see our adversity as an asset. We have become so accustomed to the comfort oriented society in which we live that any inconvenience is seen as a major trauma. We view our trials in a much different light than our advantages. Our stresses are seen as:

* The primary element for emotional strain.
* The principal reason for neurotic disorders.
* The primal attribute for functional disturbances.
* The paramount cause for interpersonal conflict!

We must see the benefits which can be derived from stress. This is the reason that the scriptures instruct: *"In everything give thanks: for this is the will of God in Christ Jesus concerning you."* - 1 Thessalonians 5:18

The next time we encounter a storm we would like to forget, it would do us all well to remember the many benefits which can be derived from a trial.

This is one key to successful living!

KEY 41   PROJECT "NEW START!"

Most people set a future starting date for that life-changing project. You have been thinking about it for years. You have wanted to do something about it for a long time. It frequently preoccupies your thoughts. You have acknowledged a need for change. On other occasions you have determined to do something about it, but this time it's different. With a gleam in your eye and a grin of determination you assert: "This time I'm going to do it ... right after Christmas!" A good time to start may be after New Year, ... on my birthday, ... in the new house, ... on my new job, ... next Summer, etc. "After all," we think, "a good project should begin on a memorable date!" But a resolution to change tomorrow, is a decision to remain the same today. "The road to Hell is paved with good intentions," said one self-perceived failure. Then he added, "and I have all the paving contracts!"

A decision to change tomorrow, is a choice to remain the same today!

The fact that the same resolves are recited every year, is proof that nothing has been done to fulfil them. A resolution is like a pan fire in the kitchen; it should be carried out immediately! If not, the consequences can be equally devastating. **Now** is the "**tomorrow**" you've been waiting for yesterday! **Today, right now** you must begin with **project new start!**

1. CANDID SELF-EXAMINATION

The starting place is with an honest self-examination. There are many hindrances to an honest self-evaluation. These include: lack of openness, integrity and candour; self-deception; a mediocre mind-set; discouragement and hopelessness. A truthful self- examination is vital for change. The scriptures command a need for self-analysis and warns of devastating consequences for those who resist:

> *"But let a man examine himself... and so let him eat of that bread, and drink of that cup. For this cause many are weak and sickly among you, and many sleep. For if we would judge ourselves, we should not be judged." - 1 Corinthians 28, 30-31*

A word study in the original Greek is most revealing. The word *weak* is *asthenio* and it means to be weary, drained, exhausted and discouraged to the point of weakness. The disciplines of mental health use the term *Asthenic Reaction* to describe this state of mind and body. The word *sick* is *aristoast* which means to be physically afflicted, ill or sickly. The word *sleep* is *koimamoi* and it means to be dead, to be placed in a state of death. The warning here is that many sincere, upright Christian people will live in discouragement, be sickly and some will die prematurely and unnecessarily. The cause is a lack of honest self-analysis. This is indeed a strong incentive for self- examination!

The word *judge* comes from the Greek word *krima* and means to go to law, to be judged, to be found guilty. The words *criminology* and *criminal* are derived from it. It suggests that we measure our behaviour and attitudes by an authoritative standard. This is why James 1:22 charges us with these words:

> *"But be ye* **doers** *of the* **word** *, and not hearers only, deceiving your own selves."*

2. A SELF-IMPROVEMENT CHECK LIST

The following Need For Self-Improvement Check List may be helpful in determining areas in your life which need to change. Tick off any of the following statements you may have made or thoughts you may have had.

Right after _____ (whatever date),   **I'm going to:**

.... Lose weight	.... Attend Church regularly
.... Get my bills paid	.... Change my attitude
.... Write those letters	.... Learn new techniques
.... Clean out my garage	..... Develop new skills
.... Sort out my files	.... Extend my aptitudes
.... Quit my vices	.... Enhance my spiritual life
.... Develop new habits	.... Correct bad relationships
.... Order my house	.... Stick to a budget
.... Organize my life	..... Control my thoughts
.... Be more hospitable	.... Develop new friendships
.... Spend more time in prayer	.... Tithe my income
.... Control my emotions	.... Other

3. JUST FOR TODAY - THINGS YOU PLAN!

Just for today, organize your life! You must **plan what you must do, then do what you have planned!**

Here is a helpful outline which will assist you in planning your day.

One day at a time. First things first! Date: _____

a) In any order, list all **See** or **Do** items for the day. Don't worry about the order. Just put them down.

b) Thoughtfully and carefully assign a priority number to each item.

c) Begin working through the list in order of priority, beginning with number 1.

d) Please note. Even though you may consider yourself to be an agnostic or sceptic, **do not skip** number 1 in your list of priorities. It will work for you!

PRIORITY	APPOINTMENT/ACTIVITY	TIME
1	Ask the Lord Jesus Christ for direction!	Morning
2		
3		
4		
5		
6		

4. PHONE CALLS TO MAKE

Work into the above schedule during a lull, or assign a priority number.

PERSON OR COMPANY	PHONE NUMBER	NOTATION

5. IDEAS AND NOTES

Ideas are flighty! Write them down, or you will lose them.

_____

_____

_____

_____

_____

_____

_____

Habitual failure is incompatible with the purposes of God! It is also an impossibility for those who maintain such a factual self-image. Whatever problem you face, you must yield yourself to God! Please do not confuse the contents of this book with "mind control," "metaphysics" or "para-psychology". What has been shared here are the basic laws of the universe, established by God. They work! Try them for yourself!

These are the keys to successful living!

FOR YOUR INFORMATION

Dr Kent is the President of the *International College of Biblical Counselling* (ICBC) and of *Turning Point Guidance and Counselling Services*. He has written a number of university level counselling courses which are available through the Directive Study Program on audio cassette. These include:

- The Well-Adjusted Personality
- The Well-Defined Philosophy
- The Exciting Marriage
- The Well-Ordered Ministry
- Peace In A Neurotic World
- Frankly Speaking (How to communicate effectively)
- The Greatest Love Story Ever Told

His books include:

- And God Said, Let There Be Sex
- Single And Happy
- I Can Change The Shape Of My World
- Frankly Speaking (How to communicate effectively)
- Climb Every Mountain
- The Greatest Love Story Ever Told

Turning Point Guidance and Counselling Services

Turning Point is a professionally operated guidance and counselling service, run as a ministry of the local church. Each counsellor is trained by the local ICBC Campus and is accountable to the church leadership.

Turning Point and ICBC operate on the premise that healing comes to the community through the local church. Our goal is to provide the teaching tools which will help the Church meet this need.

For further information, contact ICBC at the addresses and telephone numbers given in the front of the book under TWM International Publishers.